The Hero that Walks Away

Keelan LaForge

ISBN: 9798876236340

Printed in Belfast, United Kingdom.

Publisher – Independently Published

Cover Credit – james@goonwrite.com

Dedication

For all the kind-hearted Clodaghs and Jasmines of the world.

Chapter One

"Oh, Glen with the ginger hair - he has a face like a cherub."

That's what people always say about me. I've always looked younger than I am. I suppose in my forties or fifties, I'll be glad of that, but for now, I'm mistaken for a child whenever I want to do adult things. I always need to make sure my ID is close at hand; especially because I'm in a band and gigs in bars are a regular occurrence. I guess, if I'm honest, I can be like a kid at times. I had a cool job for a while, working on video games, but I left it in the end. The place shut down, so naturally, we were let go. I couldn't think of anything I wanted to do after that. I've never really had the will to work. I guess it's because I'm always hopeful that our band will take off and we'll have overnight success. I don't care if it's unlikely - it's possible, so long as we don't give up. There are four of us in the band — all best friends. Two of my pals live with each other, the remaining two of us live separately, which I think is a better idea. We already see each other in practice, so there's no point in stifling each other in our free time too. There's such a thing as too much togetherness. I know that more than anyone.

I don't do a lot with my time apart from playing in my band. It uses up all my creative energy and then I just want to relax. Still, I'm forced to go through the silly process of signing on. I'm on the dole for now, but they don't just send you money and leave you alone. You're forced to check in once every two weeks with them, to prove that you are doing your utmost to secure a job. I'm doing my utmost not to. I haven't been to an interview in months. I haven't even really bothered sending off applications recently; I just fill in the boxes in my record book and bring it to the meetings. I make up most of it and nobody seems to notice. The lady that checks mine is called Fiona. She is middle aged, stout and wears a large amount of make-up. I just play on the whole baby face thing when I'm there and she laps it up greedily. She probably has a son about my age — a sorry character that makes her entirely empathise with my plight. As far as she's concerned, I am constantly applying for work, but no one will take me on. She tells me not to worry and she doesn't put me through any gruelling questioning. She just ticks my sheet, gives me a smile and off I go, to enjoy my fortnight of funded freedom. Two weeks later, we repeat the same process. If she didn't like seeing me so much, she'd probably tick my work booklet for me, so I didn't even have to waste a morning going in. I have no reason to work; I'm working on my band and that's enough. She likes seeing me, so I'll have to keep up the routine of going in. She probably spends the meeting mentally squeezing my cheeks and thinking how adorable I am. That's the only reason I'm there.

I only get £140 every two weeks. My rent is paid by my parents, so I don't have to worry about that. It doesn't leave me much to work with, but if I can afford tobacco and papers, I'm happy. I buy cheap food as I need it and my friends and I get the odd pint, but other than that, my expenses total a round zero. I'm a person that's easily satisfied, so long as I'm not forced to do things I don't want to do. I come from a town near Glasgow, and I live in the South Side of the city. I share a modern apartment with two other guys. We barely see each other because they work so much. They both work in bartending, so they're out most nights and sleeping most days. I tend to sleep late too, but I'm up before the sun sets. They've already clocked in by then. That works well for me, because I enjoy solitude and it means I get ample alone time without anyone bothering me. People's habits tend to get to me. I don't like people that breathe loudly or noisy eaters, or anything of that nature. I don't make noise in that way, so I appreciate when others make the same effort to refrain from doing it for my sake.

I don't think I mentioned the name of my band yet. They're called *The Turnpikes*. One day, they'll be known nationally, if not internationally. I know that because we put in the work, and we're determined to succeed. That's all you need, in order to realise your dreams. The lead singer can be a bit of a knob, but we put up with him because he has charisma. He's practically tone deaf, and he doesn't know it, but he's a confident frontman, and that's the only thing you need to get anywhere in life. Sometimes, I get fed up with him. I have perfect pitch and it gets on my nerves when he's off key, but I try to ignore it because the band is my reason for living. I can't afford to get too aggravated by him. I do complain about him though; we all do – every time he hasn't arrived yet, or whenever he has already left.

I'm the rhythm guitarist and I sing backing vocals. I could probably play and sing lead, but I'm quiet and reserved and I prefer to decorate the backdrop, feeding the band my ideas and letting louder people express them for me. Sometimes they take the credit for them, and that can be annoying, but I still don't want to be front stage centre, so I put up with that.

This is going to be *The Turnpikes'* lucky year; I just know it is. We are making our own music video this year and we have the concept already figured out.

It's going to be set in a gloomy room with our shadowed figures playing dark notes. We model ourselves on post-punk, so our music tends to be slow and broody. I have written several of our songs and I love to play around with music and composition; that's where I really thrive. The video idea suits me because it means I can lurk in the background without having my face under a spotlight, but I still get to be present and enjoy the experience. After that, we might tour around the UK. We've regularly played in our own city, but never elsewhere. At least there is a post-punk scene taking off again, so I know we will draw attention. It doesn't even matter about Jake's singing. Most of those bands have singers that talk in a dull tone. It's part of the style. I keep telling myself that, so I don't get resentful that he's ruining our music.

Every member of the band has a girlfriend apart from me. It feels like everyone is in a serious relationship now. It's like an expectation that comes with being in your mid to late twenties. I've just never felt overly interested in it. Music is my love. I did have one sort-of girlfriend, briefly. I liked her because she played the guitar and she had long flowing hair, but it didn't go anywhere. We slept together once but it was underwhelming, so I never repeated the act. I see my bandmates being all smoochy with their girlfriends and I don't understand it. It makes my stomach feel like it's become one of those wibbly wobbly jellies on a plate – you know the old-fashioned kind that slips out of a mould, and it moves by its own volition – no one even needs to nudge the dish. I try not to hang around too long when it gets to that stage of the night. I just want to enjoy my pint and a good tune. I don't need to see them getting it on in the living room while I sit on my own – happily, but suddenly, noticeably alone.

I hear tunes in my head and then I transpose them on paper. I can't read music, but I draw it in a way that makes sense to my brain. I never risk forgetting the tune anyway. It circles in my head like a wasp in a jar until I let it out on my guitar strings and into my mic. The others always respond well to what I've written. I don't know if it's because they always like it, or if they're just being supportive pals. But if I didn't contribute, we'd probably have a setlist of about three songs. None of the others take it as seriously as me. They'd be happy playing covers, day in, day out. I can't think of anything worse.

The drummer is solid, but he doesn't have much input outside of keeping the beat, Jake is too busy overperforming and Greg and Mike on bass and guitar prefer to just play when they're in practice and forget about music when they aren't. I can be the quiet driving force behind this band though. That doesn't bother me; I have the passion inside me with regards to that. Mark my words, this time next year, we'll be selling out venues in London.

Chapter Two

Greg and I went for a pint at *The Box*, followed by a *Blue Lagoon* battered pizza slice. There were a few bands playing. They were mostly first timers. You could see the excitement in their faces and hear the lack of prep in their performance. I had a Guinness and listened anyway. You can learn from all music, whether you consider it to be good or bad. Even if you hate it, it reinforces what you don't want to do so you don't repeat a bad band's mistakes.

It was a Tuesday night, so it was busy, but not overwhelmingly so. We followed it with a trip to *Nice 'n' Sleazy* a few doors along. There was a good vibe in it that night. They were having an 80's night in the basement, so we headed down there for a while. It was dark and there were a lot of people swaying around to the music, drinks in hands. I felt at home there. Sometimes I think I was born to be in a basement, feeling the hum of the music vibrating through me. I could probably face working in a bar if it wasn't so problematic in that it interferes with my gig and practice schedule.

Greg slung back the pints. He's a big guy. We're the same height at over six feet tall, but he's much broader so he can really hold his drink. I tend to get pissed after a few pints and then I become really friendly and loveable, or so I've been told. I don't like the implication that I'm not that way whenever I'm sober, but I think it just becomes exaggerated when I've had a drink. It seems to go one of two ways with drinking: you either display your usual characteristics in a more pronounced way, or you become an entirely different character, unrecognisable to all who know you. I'd happily stick with the first. Greg was giving me a hard time that night, about not having a girlfriend. He says he thinks I'm gay, but I just shrug it off. It doesn't bother me when he says that. He thinks he's being funny, but I don't see sexual orientation as a laughing matter. Sometimes I wonder if I even have one at all. I can go for such extended periods without even thinking of another person, without craving their touch or warmth. I guess it's just the way I came out when I arrived in the world. I've never felt the need for it, nor have I noticed the lack of it.

He asked when I was going to get myself a girlfriend and I just shrugged. I can be honest with the guy; I've known him since we were kids.

"I'm not really interested, man."

"I've noticed. Don't you want to have someone to bring to our gigs to sing your praises?"

"No, I'm happy gigging without anyone I know watching. Not knowing the crowd makes it even better."

"That must be why you've stayed in Glasgow, you antisocial prick – it's big enough you can be as anonymous as you like and none of us can ever really pin you down."

"I'm there for every practice session, aren't I? I'm more dedicated to it than the rest of you combined."

"Fair point, man. I won't give you any more shit…today."

Greg gave me a last smirk, shook his head and looked back into his pint glass. He would have looked for his sorrows drowning in it, had he had any. But life was always peachy for him. He didn't have a care in the world, he had a girlfriend that was his best friend, and he was in an up-and-coming band. What more could he want?

"Good tune, man," he shouted as the next song started up.

It was Joy Division. Everyone knew the song, and everyone liked it – especially whenever they were drunk. They all swayed harder to it than the previous song, hands in pockets or on their pint. A few songs later, the bar called for last orders. I felt like I was just getting started. I was made to be on the road, touring and drinking into the night. Calling myself a night owl would have been a huge understatement. I was made to take flight after dark, and someday soon, I'd be flying higher than I could imagine in that moment.

Chapter Three

The next day, I got up at 1pm, made myself a leisurely fry up and an espresso and got back into bed with a book. I was reading *Murakami*. It was a tale with many turns in it. I was getting lost in the fantastic reality of it. I propped myself up on my pillow, ate my brunch and didn't make any plans to move before 7pm unless I needed the bathroom. My flatmates appeared to be in bed. The greasy smell of cooked bacon might have lured them from their beds, but I was guessing that they were in a night shift slumber, and they probably wouldn't rouse from their rooms until they had to get dressed again for work. I loved my life. I was living something close to my version of a dream life. It mightn't have been much to many people, but there were many artists that had chosen the same path. I loved living on nearly nothing and living for my art. It wasn't a sacrifice to me. It was an artist's dream. I didn't know what I would have done with extra cash, had I had it. Whenever I was working for the video game company, I was drinking away whatever I earned anyway. I hadn't noticed myself being any better off. Whenever you're working, you end up spending it all in the canteen and in the vending machines, and you go out every night of the week because you can afford to. The hangovers over your desk in work always made it feel like it wasn't worth it the next day, but somehow, I made it through. At least I didn't have to deal with that kind of post night-out regret anymore. I could do as I pleased, and I didn't have to move from my bed until practice or a gig popped up. I always found the energy for that, no matter how horrendous I might have felt immediately preceding it.

I got a text from Greg that day. He doesn't text me to chat; he just texts me to make arrangements. Like I said: he's my best friend so he knows I don't like excessive chatting. We had an early gig and then he suggested going for some drinks with a group of friends afterwards. I headed out with my beloved guitar case in my hand at 6pm. We had a two-hour session in the studio, and I couldn't wait to get cracking. I had so many ideas flooding my brain. I just hoped Jake wasn't having a particularly off-key day and that he could deliver them well and do the songs justice.

I couldn't stop with my silent judgement, try as I might. I think it might be my greatest personality flaw. Even if I really like someone, once I notice something irritating that they do, it's hard to focus on anything else. I think some people are just extra sensitive to sound. Maybe that's why I'm good at music – I notice the smallest sounds and I know how to manipulate them for good. Unfortunately, the downside to that is that I notice every cough, every tap of a pen, every intake of breath, and it really bugs me. In fact, I would go so far as to say it disturbs me.

Stevie the drummer was running late. I hated whenever late arrivals ate into our practice time. We were all paying to be there – at least – Greg was paying on my behalf that week. I hadn't had enough left to cover the cost of the session, but I'd cover him the following week when I got paid, so it was no big deal. We have a kind of brotherhood in our band that I like. Whenever you're stuck, someone will always bail you out. I've done it tens of times myself, even though I don't love doing it. I'd do anything for the band. I got my guitar plugged into my amp, got tuned and I was ready to go. I decided to show the others a few ideas that had been buzzing around in my head. I played a few parts of songs, and they all praised them – saying we'd have to work them into solid songs together. I love whenever you get that reception for something you've created. It's very rewarding and it makes up for the moments of annoyance you get – like whenever your bandmate is late for your paid time slot.

We ran through our setlist. It was pretty tight by then. We'd done it a million times and we would do it again the following night at our next gig. We had a gig lined up in a bar off Argyle Street – one we'd played in once before, so we knew the run of things. Still, you can never be overprepared for a gig, and you never know exactly who'll be in the crowd or how you'll happen to play that night.

Stevie burst through the door, effusively apologetic. He seemed genuinely upset he'd missed part of the practice. He got his cymbals out and secured them to the stands. He didn't tinker with them to check all was well; he just jumped in and played along with us. He was playing perfectly that night – I had to give him credit for that. I just don't know why people can't be on time for things that are as important as practice. We all have the same number of hours in a week, and we all have clocks that display the same time. No one else seemed bothered by his late appearance, so I tried not to let it eat away at me. I couldn't afford to let it interfere with the practice time we had left. It was so valuable and to all but me - necessary.

After we finished up the session, we walked to the pub. Greg said that his girlfriend Deborah and the rest of the girls were waiting there for us. They'd been there for a while, but they had a table saved for us, which was good. I wasn't feeling hugely social, but a few pints would correct that, no doubt. We crammed into the booth, and everyone chatted freely. I sat quietly, but not mutely. I've always been shy, but never to the point of paralysis. I can always overcome it whenever I want to do something enough.

I knew all the girls that were present, apart from one. They were the girlfriends of my bandmates, a girl that was determined to date the bassist, Evan, whether he wanted to or not, and a friend of Greg's girlfriend Deborah. Susie had red hot hair. By that I don't mean that I was attracted to her. She just had the most vivid red hair I've ever seen on a human head. My hair is red, but mine doesn't come from a bottle. It's naturally ginger. I've always had fun poked at me for being a ginger, but it's never really bothered me. Being mocked never sank into my skin; maybe I'm just not sensitive enough for it to really hurt me. Although, I know that I come across as being "sensitive." I don't know why people tend to make that assumption about me whenever they don't know me. Maybe it's the way I look; I have a baby face on a long, tall body. I'm a musician and I have my own grungy style. I like to wear plaid shirts, jeans and Doc Marten boots with matching plaid lining. Sometimes being a musician in itself is enough to cause people to make assumptions about you. "They're the musical type," people say below their breath, the same way small-minded people do when they're making homophobic or racist remarks. I've never felt like there was a perfect sized box I could slot into; I prefer to be a pile of contradictions and to keep people guessing. I'm glad I'm not sensitive; it looks like it must be a strain. I don't tend to overthink about anything, despite the impression I seem to put across.

The new girl in our midst did intrigue me. I couldn't compare her to anyone I'd met before. She had unkempt hair in a grey-blonde shade and eyes of watery blue. She was very quiet, and I wondered what she was thinking about for a minute. Then I got involved in talking about the band and that thought disappeared. It was my priority over all else, which I'm sure you realise by now.

We had a few pints and listened to *Toots and the Maytals*. It was a place where I hoped we would get the chance to play. It was on my bucket list – not the far-reaching end of it, just somewhere I wanted to check off the list, and soon. It had tropical décor and lighting that made it look like prime sunbathing time in the Caribbean – not that I've ever done that or ever would. I have typically pale Scottish skin. It burns as soon as the sun's rays glaze its surface. It's probably a good thing I live in such a shitty climate. It rains day in, day out.

11

Sun is only ever like an exclamation mark inserted at the end of a long sentence, and I've never been a fan of the overuse of exclamation marks. Why do people have to get so excited about everything? I get excited about things worth getting excited about – a gig, the prospect of a tour, a recording session, but not about the silly, trivial things other people waste their energy on, like love.

Chapter Four

After a few drinks, it was suggested that we go back to Mike's flat for a few more drinks. He said he had some beers in the fridge, and he was happy to share. It was a pretty tight squeeze, but we all found somewhere to sit and a glass to drink out of. There was an iPod dock sitting out on the kitchen table, so I took charge of it. I carry my iPod with me wherever I go. Those were the days before smartphones did everything: the year of 2011. I scrolled through my playlists, picking my favourite one at that current moment. I stayed near the music station, waiting to flick songs if needs be. Everyone else was busy talking, and there was enough of a murmur in the room without me contributing to it. We needed a DJ and no one else was taking care of that.

The girl with the wild hair was sitting cross-legged beside her flatmate. She was silent and she looked like she was concentrating on something. I wondered what she was thinking about and why she wasn't as loud as her friends. They were all shouting each other down, telling anecdotes as a group, filling in the blanks for whoever hadn't been there at the time.

I put my favourite Bruce Springsteen track on and sat down near the girl whose name I didn't know.

"I love this Springsteen song," she said.

It was like she'd written me a personalised love letter. Her words were poetic lyrics to my sensitive ears.

"You know this?" I asked, in disbelief.

"Yeah, it's not like his other stuff – it's more bluesy – that's why I like it," she said.

"Do you like blues?" I asked.

"Yeah, it's my favourite – the sixties was my favourite decade for music."

"Oh, you're the one..." I said, remembering a comment Susie with the poker red hair had made about her flatmate.

"Susie said you were obsessed with the sixties, and hippies."

"Yes," she smiled.

"Do you like music in general?"

"Yeah, but I'm picky about what I listen to – very picky. I don't like any of the stuff you'd hear on the radio."

"Me neither."

It felt like I had an instant connection with her. We were bound together by music, and I couldn't stop talking to her. Ordinarily, I would have walked away by then to search for the next track I wanted to play, but I just let my iPod do the work for itself. It only had good tunes on it anyway. I wouldn't have added anything to do it that hadn't passed my scrutiny and my careful selection process.

It turned out the girl's name was Clodagh, and she came from the Republic of Ireland: Wicklow. She had moved to Glasgow for university, and she had studied English, she said. She'd graduated a couple of months earlier. She planned on becoming an English teacher. She had already started her teaching course, and she wanted to stay in Glasgow for good. She'd been there for years, and she'd fallen in love with the place. She said it had taken a while, but by then, she'd been there so long that it felt like it had always been home. She still sounded very Irish to me. It was something a bit different. I've always liked things that are a bit different.

We talked for what felt like mere minutes, but it was more likely to have been hours. I didn't want the night to end. I've never felt that way about talking to someone. I'm usually secretly relieved whenever I get back to my room, pull the duvet over myself and light a cig. My ashtray has been a far better companion to me than any person ever has, and I have had a couple of good friends – the kind of friends that would do anything for you. But whenever you have that kind of friend, it tends to make you lazy about what you're willing to do back. You sit back and wait to be served without consciously deciding to – they just set the precedent for it by over-giving.

Eventually, Abigail and her pals decided it was time to head home. I walked Clodagh to the door, hesitated, leant in and gave her a kiss on the cheek. Everyone sang "aww," and I could feel myself reddening. I do get embarrassed easily which is made more obvious by the red flush that comes to my pale face. I've never been one for romantic gestures, but she inspired it in me. I wished she could stay longer and that we could have a cuddle. I'm generally not a cuddly person, so it was surprising to me that I wanted to.

We looked at each other tenderly and smiled and then her friends took her by the arm and led her out the door. I could hear them giggling in the hallway. Everything echoes in those tenement hallways. I didn't give it much more thought after that. I guess I'm just somebody that lives in the moment.

Chapter Five

Tracy was one of Deborah's friends that had been there that night. She's always been quite forthcoming. She tells you things you don't want to know without you having to ask. I suppose there are times when it can be helpful to have someone so straight-talking around. You never have to wonder what she thinks of someone. She's uninhibited about sharing her opinions. She's just one of those loud, jovial types that you can hear talking from a mile away. You could quote her word for word without even being in the same street. She approached me by text, in the usual way in which she barges in. I was still in bed, and I was nursing a bit of a hangover. I had no need to get up, but my headache had woken me anyway. I had band practice, but not until the evening, so I had a long period of recovery ahead of me first. My phone sounded and I picked it up. I'm not much of a phone person, so it was unusual for me to read or reply to a message as soon as it came through.

"You and Clodagh seemed to get on well last night. Do you want me to send you her number?"

I pondered it for a moment and then I told her to tell Clodagh to contact me through Facebook. The feeling I'd had after a couple of drinks had worn off and I felt unmotivated and like sleep was luring me back into laziness. I succumbed to it and had a rest for a few more hours. Whenever I woke up again, a message awaited me in which I received a scolding from Tracy for not being more proactive, but she told me she'd passed the message on to Clodagh.

An hour or so later, I checked my Facebook, merely out of interest. At that stage, everyone was on it all the time. It was the star of the social media show. I talked to friends on it, saw their updates and shared relevant content. It hadn't been overrun with ads yet. In effect, I still checked it as regularly as I would my email. It wasn't out of pure eagerness for a message. That wasn't because I had no interest in Clodagh either; I've just always been content on my own. In the sober light of day, I didn't feel as affectionate as I had whenever I had a few drinks in me. I just wanted to lie in bed, go to practice, lie in bed, go to practice, maybe read a few books and have a few pints, smoke myself silly. I was satisfied with that lifestyle. Clodagh's message had arrived. I opened it up and it was quite concise.

"Hi, Tracy said to get in touch with you. It was nice meeting you last night."

I replied to her. I've always been told to be polite. That's one of the qualities I think people like about me. I was raised to never leave a message unanswered and to always be on time for things. Whenever you check those two things off the list, people tend to miss the fact that you're lacking other important characteristics. Politeness covers up a lot of other failings.

I opened my *Murakami* novel and got lost in the world he created for our enjoyment and for our confusion. I love whenever a story transports you to a world where you forget your own — where the bounds of truth and fantasy melt away. I lay there for a long time, until I felt my body calling for an espresso and some food. Cigarettes are always my breakfast. I have an ashtray on my bedside table. I'm pretty religious about emptying it. I always attend to the things that are priorities for me. I rolled a few smokes, and I had another one, pulling the smoke into my lungs hungrily and letting it go with all my might. It was all I needed in that moment; there was nothing else missing. I had no feelings of discomfort or lack.

After a while, I got myself a coffee. The coffee maker belongs to my flatmate Bill, but he told us to use it as if it was our own. I think I'm the only regular coffee drinker in the apartment anyway. I made myself some fried food. I love anything cooked to a crisp in oil. I'm one of those people that never puts on weight. I could eat day and night and my shape would still resemble that of a string bean. I might be tall and skinny, but I wouldn't change it. I like being able to eat unhealthily and to have no consequences, other than the greasy odour that clings to the walls of the apartment afterwards. The place already smells of cigarettes, so that doesn't bother me. They're my two favourite smells, in fact. The guys never complain about either of them. We are all equally easy going and that works out well.

I went for a hot shower and got dressed in my usual type of outfit: plaid shirt in burgundy tones, dark jeans and the ring I wore on my finger. It didn't have any real sentimental value. I had bought it on holiday, and it had wild animals carved into it. I've just worn it for so many years that it has become one with my finger. I have a habit of swivelling it round whenever I'm sitting idly. It's not a nervous habit, like some people might suppose. I just do it because I can't get my hands on my guitar, and I guess they are used to playing around on it. I have busy fingers and a busy brain when it comes to song writing. I think that might be why I'm so lethargic the rest of the time. I direct all my energy into that, so there's nothing left for anything else.

I lazed about with my book, replying to Clodagh's messages whenever she replied to me. We had plenty to talk about; she was a chatty girl even though she was quiet and softly spoken, and I found her incredibly easy to talk to. It helped that she adored music. She used to play in bands herself, she told me. I was glad she wasn't in one at that moment, because I might have felt competitive about that. I want to be the main musician – the one that realises their dream of fame and fortune. I know that I'll eventually have to leave Glasgow to do that, but I don't think far ahead; I don't even think about next week. When you live like I do, you have to live for the moment you're in. That's what enables me to accept my small dole payments with grace. I'm not rich, but I feel like I am on the day I receive it. I always treat myself to a new packet of tobacco and some delicious food. I go for a pint or two and I pay for the practice room whenever I can – and I'm as happy as a grinning cartoon clam. Nothing could enhance that feeling, other than "making it" with the band on the level I aspire to.

Clodagh and I agreed to meet up again, alone. I couldn't do it that day, but we arranged to get a drink a couple of days later. I was excited to see her, which was strange. It wasn't a feeling I was used to getting. I could feel a sensation like bubbles rising and popping inside my stomach. I wondered if those were the butterflies that everyone always talked about experiencing; I never had before. It did feel good. It was like the rush you get when a good pint and a good song converge and you're in your own kind of heaven, usually found in the darkest of bars.

Practice was frustrating that night. I went there filled with enthusiasm, like a balloon swelling to capacity, but it instantly deflated whenever I walked through the door. Jake was singing into his mic, and he was ridiculously off-key. The sound grated on me like a lawn mower on a Saturday morning. I had to bite my tongue, just so I didn't say something rude to him. I wanted to single-handedly kick him out of the building, but we didn't have a back-up vocalist and I wasn't ready to offer to step forward, so I endured it, as always. Sometimes, I dreamed of sending Jake packing before we tried to embark on a tour. But however hopeless he might have been as a singer, we had made a pact as a band: we all made it or none of us did. None of us could be replaced: we were a band of friends before we were a band of musicians – at least, that was what the others felt. Sometimes, I wanted to perform a ruthless cull, but the drummer and I would have been the only two left, and we're both pretty quiet guys. Maybe every band needs to have someone loud and obnoxious, to play to the crowd – even if they're talentless as far as the music is concerned.

We worked through our setlist and once we got into it, things improved. We've run through it so many times now that it's like second nature to us – to me anyway. Whenever our time was up, I felt ready to go home and retreat to my room, to hide in my bed for twelve hours and rest. Band life was beautiful, but sometimes it was brutal too.

Chapter Six

Clodagh and I met in a bar close to her flat. I suggested it to be a gentleman, like my parents trained me to be. It was a cool place too. I'd always liked the vibe of the place. It felt like a German beer bar, with its light wooden interior and its tankards decoratively placed on shelves. They had every uncommon beer you could think of, and it was quiet enough inside that you could have a conversation without straining your voice.

Clodagh was beautiful. I had to admit that. She was classically pretty, but with wild hair. I liked the fact it made her stand out as being different to the typical girl I met. Anyone I knew had limp, straight locks that they struggled to get any volume into. Her hair had a life force of its own. I just wanted to run my hands through it and to play with it. She was wearing a red velvet dress with white ruffles around the collar. She looked like she'd stepped into my world from a different era – and maybe she'd return to her own at the end of the evening. There was something almost unrealistic about her. She belonged in black and white film. I couldn't stop staring at her, even though I never normally feel compelled to do that. We got two high stools at the window and our knees brushed against each other's below the counter. We were overlooking the street, but it was dark, and you couldn't see much: just a few headlights shining through the persistent rain. It was falling without intermission and the cars were spreading puddles vertically every time they passed by. I could see our reflections in the wet windows, and we looked good together. We almost looked like we fitted perfectly together. In that moment, I didn't know why I couldn't find the oomph to contact her first. I could have made more of an effort to communicate with her first, but I had lost enthusiasm for it after that first night. Maybe I tend to forget people quickly. Whenever they're seated in front of me, I might be struck by them, but whenever they go away, the distance becomes like a cavity in my mind that all their forgotten characteristics fall into. Out of sight, out of mind – that's the phrase that covers it best – however clichéd it may be.

Conversation flowed so easily with Clodagh. There was never a moment's awkward silence between us. Her warm smile made me feel comfortable with her. She was welcoming even whenever she didn't utter a word. We gazed into each other's eyes longingly, which was something I had never experienced before. My eyes jumped between each of her features, drawn in by every one of them. They were all so beautiful I couldn't settle on one. I really liked her – I knew that then. It wasn't just a one-off moment fuelled by drink; I had genuinely liked her when I had given her a peck on her cheek that first night in the flat.

We talked about everything and nothing. I couldn't have provided a summary of what was said at the end of the night; I was just impressed with a feeling that I knew I couldn't forget. Clodagh smoked with enthusiasm. That made her even better in my eyes. I didn't have to try to justify my habit, or pretend I was going to eventually give it up; I could just be myself with her. At regular intervals, we went outside and stood in the rain, facing one another, sharing a cigarette – momentary joy under the insistent rain that thundered down with grim inevitability.

A homeless man approached us as we stood there, asking for some spare change. I shook my head, but Clodagh reached into her bag, pulled out her purse and gave him the change she had. He nodded at her in gratitude and backed away, holding the precious metal in his grubby, clenched hand.

"Why did you do that?" I demanded. I felt angry about it. She was compromising her safety for the sake of an old drunk. Worse than that – it was unsanitary.

"I just feel bad for him, and for anyone that's homeless."

"He probably has a nicer house than either of us do. You do know he's only going to use it for drink?" I asked.

She smiled at me. She seemed to understand that I was being protective of her. It wasn't that I was mean with money – it was that I wanted her to be sensible on the streets of Glasgow. She still seemed naïve to me – like someone that hadn't grown up in the city. Maybe her own hometown just had a different feel to it, or maybe she just had an incredibly kind heart. I couldn't say I related to that, even though I knew it was an admirable quality to have, in theory.

She put her purse back inside her bag and zipped it up for good measure under my watchful eye. We walked back into the bar. I placed my hand in the small of her back as she walked. She had a curvature in her spine that was like the classic Coke bottle shape. I wondered what she looked like without clothing on. That wasn't even a regular consideration of mine. They say that men are always thinking about sex and nudity, but not me. It's just not something that crops up a lot for me. Yes, I get aroused, but it isn't something I feel every minute of the day, and I can live without satisfying whatever urges creep in. Still, Clodagh stirred something inside me, and I felt curious about her body and the details of it that made it unique. Her hair was long and flowing and it tickled the back of my hand as she turned around to face me. I thought she was going to kiss me, but she held back. Maybe she was waiting for me to make the first move. So, I tilted my head and moved in. She was warm and welcoming, and her mouth tasted like strawberry beer. She'd been drinking it for the last hour, so it made sense that it did, but there was something intoxicating about it that I hadn't expected. It felt like I couldn't get enough of that taste. I imagined she tasted like strawberries even whenever she hadn't been consuming them. That somehow felt completely plausible.

Last orders hadn't been called yet, but I needed to make my way home to the South Side of the city before the subway closed. I walked Clodagh back to her flat. It was only a few feet from the bar anyway. I left her on the doorstep. We kissed and I felt the ghost of that kiss lingering on my lips for a long time afterwards. It would be nice to see her again, but I didn't feel the pressing need to arrange anything. I had band practice the next few nights and she didn't seem like the type to initiate another meeting. She'd probably wait around for ever without complaint until I suggested our next date.

I descended the escalator that fed into the mouth of the subway. It was empty inside. I was the only one there. There weren't even any loitering drunks. I walked to the platform I needed and waited for the echoing rattle of the approaching train. I felt an ache that I wasn't used to; I realised I was disappointed to leave her.

Chapter Seven

I wrote a couple of songs. They were masterful and original in every way. I knew the others in the band would love them, but would they fully appreciate what they contained? It didn't feel like they had a well-developed appreciation for music; they just liked a good tune when they heard it. This had different dynamics and key changes; something I knew Jake's voice couldn't adequately convey. It felt like I was sacrificing my children to a pack of starved wolves, but there was no other option. Sometimes, I dreamt of leaving the band. I dreamt of joining a group of talented musicians and making a fresh start, but it was too much of a gamble. How could I guarantee I'd end up in a better band than the one I was in? What if I met spectacular musicians that just never got any sort of acclaim? Sometimes the fame people find has nothing to do with being the best; it's just being in the right place at the right time, and sometimes that can even be with the wrong musicians.

Whenever I had finished songwriting, I replied to Clodagh. She said she was in bed. She had given her teaching course a miss that day. She said she was ill, but I thought it was probably a hangover. She said it was the flu. We talked on and off all day, but I was often slow to respond. Like I said, I'm not one of those people that lives through their phones. I prefer the physical world and the things I'm doing to conversations over the past, future, or detailing everything I'm doing in the current moment. I want to do things that benefit me; I don't want to waste time talking about doing them.

I made myself some square sausage sandwiches and lounged around in my room. *Murakami* was reaching the end, and I was ready to start another one. Sometimes it felt like he was the only writer I connected with. Very few things touch me, especially whenever it comes to the words of others, but his were unique enough that I truly valued them. I felt like they were feeding my music, inspiring me to write things that were entirely different to my usual efforts. Isn't that the definition of great art?

I think that some people are born to be artists and others are born to be ordinary. I could never be satisfied with an ordinary life: a beige job, a beige house, a beige partner and black and white bills. I need to be able to pick myself up and go wherever I like, whenever I like, even if I never go anywhere. It's knowing it's a possibility that makes everything feel bearable. I know I'm not the only person ever to have felt that way. There are people trapped in places they don't want to be over the entire surface area of the Earth, but their dreams keep them alive and moving forwards.

I remembered about Clodagh then, and the fact it was my turn to text her back. She mightn't have been my biggest dream in life, but she was something that offset the disappointment of not being exactly where I wanted to be by then. I thought about her strawberry scent and her fierce mane, and I wanted to see her again. Well, later in the week, at least.

Chapter Eight

I took Clodagh to a Blues night in the city centre. She constantly told me how much she loved Blues music; it was her favourite. She had a record player and she listened to all the blues rock legends on it on a loop. That intrigued me. I didn't even have a record player, but she told me that she had gone to Edinburgh to pick it up. That was a real devotion to music, I thought. Granted, it was only fifty minutes on the train, but it was still an effort to source something she probably could have got closer to home. Most girls I'd met before her spent their money on Cava and clothes. Clodagh clearly liked clothes too, but her personality was much more developed than most of the people I had met. I liked the fact she was complex, and it felt like you could strip away layers of her and always find another layer underneath. I like mysteries that are hard to solve. It keeps the mind active and that's important for the creative process.

We met at the bar and walked inside, hand in hand. She took my hand first, but I didn't mind being physical with her. Ordinarily, it was unwanted, and it made me feel uncomfortable, but with her, it was different. Maybe it was because I knew she existed on a different level to most. She wasn't in pursuit of superficial things. She certainly wasn't put off by the fact that I was a struggling musician. She didn't seem to be interested in money and she didn't expect me to pay for every one of her drinks, but I still tried to offer to get her one. She motivated me to do that, at least.

The bands that were playing that night all depressed me in a way. They were all well into their sixties and they were highly skilled musicians. They were probably getting paid to play, but not enough. That wasn't their reason for being there. They just loved to perform, and they loved playing the Blues. It was a listening kind of evening. Clodagh was quiet and respectful of the music and that made me think even more highly of her. She was proving me wrong about romance. I'd always thought of it as something frivolous, but she did inspire romantic feelings in me. I just worried that they weren't strong enough for her. She seemed like such a passionate creature, and I've always been lukewarm about everything but music. I got enough out of her company that I was prepared to pursue a relationship, so long as it didn't interfere with my music. I didn't think it ever would because she had such a deep reverence for the world of music. If she didn't, we wouldn't have been sitting there in silence, contemplating every note.

We talked between songs and there was an ease between us. I don't believe in soulmates, or in fate; I believe in science and things with proof to substantiate them. But there was just an effortlessness that made spending time together easy. Otherwise, I wouldn't have put up with it. I never do anything I can't be bothered to do. My parents always said that about me whenever I lived with them. I suppose they know me as well as anybody does.

One Blues staple came after another and I knew all of them, but not as well as Clodagh did. She didn't listen to much else and she knew every inflection and every lyric. I was falling for the musician in her, but not the human in her. I could see that she was passionate in a way that extended far beyond music, and I couldn't relate to that. But she was funny. Maybe it was her Irish accent combined with her drole delivery, but she made me laugh a lot. A good laugh is enough to get me to stick around for a while. Most people want love; I want entertainment and mental stimulation.

Whenever I observed Clodagh, I knew that she was striking. She had fine features, and she looked a bit like a china doll but she had her own style too. She wore Docs like mine, with a different plaid interior. I would have worn her boots if they'd fitted me. She had excellent taste. She was wearing a white cotton dress with little rose buds printed on it. It felt crisp to the touch, like it had never been worn before and it was obviously great quality. I appreciate things like that. It's hard to find clothing as well made as that, especially these days. Most people I meet wear quick turnover stuff from chain stores: one wear and it's finished. It might as well be a single use plastic bag. Clodagh had a true appreciation for the things that mattered to me.

A Peter Green cover came on and Clodagh lit up all over. It was like the song illuminated her from the inside out. She told me how much Peter Green meant to her. She could relate to him because he was so sensitive, and he'd had such a tough life. She told me he had retreated from public life and sold all his possessions at one point, choosing to lead the existence of a pauper without being prompted to do so. I liked hearing stories about musicians getting by on very little, especially famous ones. It made it feel like my dream of "making it" was within reach, and even if I couldn't fund it, it didn't matter. You could make life up as you went along, like adding squares to a patchwork quilt, making it bigger each time you thought you were finished with the original design. It was ever-changing and ever-expanding.

Clodagh rested her head on my shoulder and something inside me felt like it was melting. I couldn't identify the feeling, but it reminded me of a chocolate bombe – structured on the outside, warm and runny on the inside. She stirred something in me; that much was sure. But I couldn't be sure of what it was. I could only be sure of the setting we were in and the music we were listening to. I knew every note intimately, even though I had never put them together in a sequence like that. It was like jazz; I could appreciate it from afar, but it wasn't my chosen genre. The guys on stage looked like they were winding down. That's the problem with performing in old age, I think; you can't have the same stamina. The guy at the mic was trying to be cool; but that was exactly how it came across: like he was trying and not quite making it there. They all wore suits with red ties, and they had patchy, grey hair and liver spots. It was hard to rock hard with guys that looked like they were ready to check into a care home, but I could still appreciate their musicianship and their devotion to the craft. One day, they must have been something special. It motivated me to make sure that our band made it whenever we were still young. I didn't want to perform in pubs and at weddings at the age of seventy, struggling to support the weight of my guitar.

I didn't know what Clodagh wanted out of life – at least not long term. I hadn't bothered to ask her. It didn't really matter in the grand scheme of things. I would be on the road in a few years, and I knew I wouldn't want to be tied to anyone then. It wouldn't be fair on them, and I couldn't promise that I'd ever return. Being on the road sounded to me like most people's marital bliss probably sounded to them. I was made to keep moving.

Chapter Nine

I went back to Clodagh's flat that night. I'd been in it before. I went to a party there a year earlier, and it turned out Clodagh had been invited too. But we hadn't crossed paths, unlikely as it sounds. It had been a busy party, and it was an exceptionally big apartment. She lived in a tenement building beside the subway station, so it was perfect for easily coming and going. I knew I could make a quick escape if I needed to – and it was likely that I would. I just got a feeling that rose inside me – an immediate aversion to the person whose company I was in. I've always had a low tolerance for romance, so maybe that was all it was. Even with my best friends, I quickly reach my limit. I like being alone. Most people don't understand that because they get lonely. I have no idea what loneliness feels like. I could probably stay in a single room for the rest of my life. So long as I had my guitar and my music, I'd be happy.

Clodagh's flatmates were easy to get along with. It helped that I'd known Susie for a couple of years. We'd never spent any one-on-one time together, but she was a friendly person and she never let an awkward silence settle. Her other flatmate was a girl called Sarah. She worked in the same place as Susie, which didn't seem to prevent them spending time together in their free time. They were always together, apart from whenever they closed the doors to their own bedrooms. The flat was just as messy as ours. The kitchen was a pigsty, but I didn't mind – so long as I could make myself an espresso there. They had a stove top espresso maker, so I helped myself to a coffee each time I arrived in the afternoon. I didn't offer one to anyone else. It only held enough coffee for one, so there was no point in offering.

That night, I was pretty intoxicated. I've never been able to hold my drink well compared to my pals. Maybe it's because I'm so skinny. Clodagh and I sat in the living room for a while, listening to her music on the iPod dock. We got under the duvet they used instead of central heating. They had gas heating, but it was always shut off to save money. It was a typical broke graduates' flat. The place did have a chill, mainly because of the high ceilings and the sheer size of the rooms. My modern place held heat better. But our bodies were quickly pressed together. Clodagh and I lay the length of the sofa with her lying flat on top of me. We kissed for a long time and my hands explored her body. I was turned on even though I had my doubts about whether I was capable of that feeling. Maybe it was just testament to how attractive she was. She was one of a kind, and I knew that. I could date for the rest of my life, and I'd never meet someone as exceptional as her again. It was like I'd discovered a rare artifact, but maybe I wasn't the right person to treasure it. I might have known it was costly and unique, but it wasn't my area of expertise. Never mind owning it, I didn't know if I even wanted to spend significant time in the museum that displayed it.

Clodagh kissed me lengthily and I felt her body heat combining with mine. It was comforting in a way, being that physically close to someone. I'd only ever experienced it once before. Maybe the even coldest of us need some human warmth sometimes. I've always thought of myself as being that way: cold. I know it's probably not widely recognised as a desirable characteristic, but it has never bothered me. Maybe that's something that goes along with being cold: the not caring. Clodagh was the opposite to that; I could see that. She was kind, caring and tender on the inside. Maybe, I thought, if I spent enough time with her, she would transmit some of that feeling to me. In the meantime, I lay back, enjoyed the physical feelings and responded appropriately.

After spending an hour on the sofa, we decided to move into the bedroom. It felt like it was only a matter of time until someone walked in on us, even though we'd been lucky enough to have the room to ourselves all evening. There was no sound in the flat, and no visible life about the place: maybe her flatmates were staying out late. They were noisy, so their arrival was always obvious. I followed Clodagh into her bedroom. The room fitted her bohemian style. There were red curtains that framed the tall window, a full bookcase, lots of knickknacks, an incense burner, fairy lights, and everything else I associated with her style. It was thoughtfully put together, like everything else about her. The record player sat on the floor beside her desk. It was a long, narrow room, but she made it cosy, and it wasn't as vast as the living room. The living room had three sofas and several armchairs sitting in it, and it still looked empty. It was painfully cold, but Clodagh's room was strangely temperate.

We kissed until we were lying on her bed, and then we got undressed. I didn't feel awkward being naked in front of Clodagh. She didn't seem to feel that way with me either. It felt natural and right. I studied her body from head to foot.

"You're the hottest woman I've ever seen," I said.

I could see her glowing from my compliment. Surely, she should have been used to it? It was a wonder that she'd been single when we'd met. The only thing that made sense was that she was over-eager and emotionally attached and it scared some people away. It probably would have scared me away too, had I not been immune to the transmission of others' feelings. I was able to take the good qualities and to leave the bad behind – like people pick and choose options at an all you can eat buffet.

We slept together and then it began to feel like she was somehow wrapping her tendrils around me. It was a feeling that made me extremely uncomfortable, but I didn't share that information with her. Afterwards, she looked blissfully happy, lying beside me. She probably thought we were building a bond. It was sad, really. I lit a cigarette and lay back, sending puffs of smoke into the atmosphere. My cigarette made me happier than any person ever could have. I could hear the traffic outside and I listened to it – it gave me a vague sense of comfort. Some things never change, even when you aren't alone in your own room. Soon enough, I would be.

Chapter Ten

I was invited to a dinner party. If I'm honest, I didn't want to go. It sounded like a lot of effort, socially - more than I was willing to make. I'm a creature of habit. I like to stick with my friends that I already know well and with family I've known my whole life. I'm not hugely keen on meeting new acquaintances. I can't remember the last time that I met one and they became a close friend. Closeness is relative to whomever the closeness concerns. My idea of closeness might be entirely different from yours, or from the person beside you, or the person on the direct opposite point of the globe. I like a bit of affection when I'm drunk and that satisfies me for a while. I can get by on limited interactions and limited touch. Others are clingier. I've seen it time and time again. I can't change myself to suit them. I've never really considered doing it anyway. Why would I? I can't understand why anyone would do that. If there's a mismatch, it's too much effort to try to make it fit together. It's like forcing a puzzle piece into the wrong hole. It doesn't matter how much determination you put into it; it's never going to fit — not without getting damaged and ruining the look of the picture, at least.

Clodagh asked me to go to the dinner party. She told me that her flatmates' boyfriends would be there, and she didn't want to be a fifth wheel. I didn't feel like we made a complete pair anyway. I was a sixth wheel on a car that only ever needed four. She should probably just have followed them on her own bike. Despite my views, whenever she appeals to me to do something for her, there's something in me that automatically agrees to it. Maybe it's the way she poses the question; it's so pleasant you can't see a way around saying yes. She has long curled eyelashes too and she has a special way of fluttering them when she wants something from someone. It's probably not even conscious, and it's surprising that something so simply flirtatious works, but it does. There must be some part of me that can't let go of trying to please her even though I know it's impossible to do so long-term.

So, I went to the dinner party, and it was bearable, mainly thanks to the cooking. The three girls had been prepping food all day. We had a huge roast dinner to celebrate the arrival of Halloween. They were all in costume and you could tell they'd planned it all out. I was wearing my usual clothing. Getting dressed up was too much effort. Thankfully, the other guys hadn't bothered getting dressed up either. It's not something I could ever be bothered doing —

whatever the occasion. I wandered into the kitchen to say hello to Clodagh and her flatmates. They were dressed as the three witches from *Hocus Pocus*, and they were sweating over steaming pots. I just wanted to settle down with a smoke and listen to some music. I took charge of the unmanned dock and put on a playlist I knew I'd enjoy even if no one else did.

I sat in the armchair and chatted to Simon, Sarah's boyfriend. He was an alright guy. He didn't talk too much and whenever he did, he didn't waste any words on useless conversation. He could be funny after a few drinks as well. He practically lived in the flat, from what I'd seen. He was there almost every time I visited. Clodagh didn't seem put out by his presence. She was more irritated by her other flatmate's boyfriend. She said he left his shoes outside her door, so she tripped over them every time she got up for work. I don't think I'm that kind of inconsiderate – I might be a bit self-centred, but I have the decency to not leave my boots sitting in places where others might trip on them. Some people are just selfish and obnoxious. Some people are hard to like.

We ended up receiving a huge meal. We had a roast dinner with all the trimmings. The flatmates had made red cabbage in a sauce with Christmassy spices enhancing it. I've never been keen on cabbage, but I enjoyed it. It seemed that they'd spent all day, gathered around their cauldron in the kitchen, cooking. I thought that was something women had fought for the right not to do, but there was something nurturing about them, and it was a compliment knowing they had gone to that amount of effort for us. Clodagh asked me what I thought of my meal, and I complimented it. I didn't go overboard with my praise, but I gave enough that I could see her lighting up a little. I could see how happy I made her, by doing very little: just by being myself and saying something to make her smile. She was very pretty when she smiled; she had an angelic sort of look, and it seemed like every part of her became luminescent whenever she was contented. Anyone else would have fully appreciated that kind of beauty before them, but it was a little wasted on me. I knew I should want it more than I'd ever wanted anything in my life, but my guitar meant more to me; I couldn't help it; that's just the way I am.

We sat around the table, talking into the next day. The pumpkins caved in on themselves from the heat of the candles. The music was changed multiple times, becoming more and more insufferable as we moved through every taste at the table. It's hard to find someone with the same taste in music as you. That was one of the things that was so amazing about Clodagh. She mightn't have had my exact taste in music, but I respected the music she did like. It had laid the groundwork for other great artists that came after it. I could listen to it and appreciate it for what it was. It wasn't like a lot of the bland, generic radio music most other people I met listened to. Clodagh left the table and didn't return. It took about twenty minutes for me to realise that she mightn't emerge from the bedroom again.

Whenever I joined her, I was ready to remove myself for the night too. It was 4am and I had identified what I disliked about everyone in the room hours earlier. There's such a thing as too much company, even if it's good company. Clodagh had reached her limit too. She was lying on the bed, looking weary and anxious. I lay beside her and hugged her. She didn't need to explain to me why she had removed herself; I completely understood it. In that way we were very much alike. If only that could make me feel something stronger for her. We slept until lunchtime the next day. When we awoke, we could hear all the noise carrying in from the café downstairs. There were a couple of kids whining and I was so glad I didn't have to deal with one of my own, or any of my friends'.

"Wah," I mimicked the sound, scrunching up my face like a petulant toddler.

Clodagh laughed hysterically at me.

"You actually look like a baby having a tantrum," she said.

"It must be the baby face thing," I shrugged, lighting myself a cigarette.

"Do it again!" she cheered, like an overexcited toddler herself.

"Wah," I repeated, in the most babyish voice I could muster with exaggerated expression.

She laughed in delight. You couldn't help but enjoy her youthful energy. Granted, at twenty-four she wasn't old, but she had the fun energy of a kid. At least she was able to switch it on and off though; she could be serious whenever appropriate, or sometimes, too serious when I wished she wouldn't take something I'd done with such gravity.

I lay in bed, sucking on my cigarette.

"That's so funny," she said. "Would you ever have a kid?"

"Not any time soon. Why, would you?" I asked in horror.

I tried to make it sound neutral, but I didn't quite manage it. I couldn't understand how someone our age could even contemplate it. There was too much beautiful freedom and too little responsibility to tempt me into ruining it with children.

"Yeah, I would."

"Like, now?" I asked, horrified. I couldn't hide my shock.

"Not now but I wouldn't want to wait for a very long time."

I guess she had that biological clock issue that I didn't have, but I didn't think I'd ever want kids. I didn't want to break it to her, but I thought I'd rather save myself the drama and save her the upset of revealing my cards; even though we were playing a game she was always going to lose in the end, unbeknownst to her.

We lay there lazily for a while and then I got up to go to the French café around the corner. The place sold amazing handmade pizzas and sandwiches. We had a shared addiction to them. That was one thing we truly bonded over. That's the kind of thing that connects me to others: food. It's like a good cigarette or a good song. The pleasure it brings you is immediate, and you want someone to share it with for a joint or collective appreciation of it. It's like having a joint, except I don't get to do that often because I rarely have the cash for it. Maybe whenever we are on tour, the opportunity will present itself more often.

I brought Clodagh her lunch. She got her favourite baguette, and I got mine. We had a coffee each too. It was predictably delicious. I could have eaten every meal in that café, could I have afforded it. It was good value for such high-quality food. It was all freshly made and authentically French and you could get a filled baguette for under a fiver. As soon as we finished eating and mopped up our mess with many napkins, I didn't hesitate in announcing my departure and headed for the subway. Clodagh offered to walk me there, but I refused. There was no point in dragging the whole thing out for the sake of a walk that would only take me two minutes alone. I descended into the subway station, and I felt a wave of relief wash over me. I was alone and I was safe again.

Chapter Eleven

Clodagh was getting increasingly upset with me and I didn't know how to avoid it. I tried to talk her down when she became distressed, but her emotions were so strong I didn't know what to do with them. I guess it'd be like giving a baby to a selfish bachelor and expecting him to know what to do whenever he's never given a thought to another person in his entire existence. Having self-awareness doesn't always make you a better person though; some people don't want to change or can't. I knew she deserved the best of the best, but I was giving my all and it wasn't enough for her.

I asked her if I could call over to see her after practice and a few drinks. With alcohol in my system, the warmth of her bed and the comfort of her hugs sounded alluring. She was quick to respond in the affirmative. She always was. It was like she was waiting by the phone, willing me to offer to see her. There was something about that that put me off whenever I was sober, but when I was drunk, I felt just as affectionate as her. I became like a favoured teddy bear, and I was happy to be cuddled and smothered – until I sobered up again, at least. In the cool clarity that morning brought, it became repulsive.

When I got to her flat, it was much later than I'd intended. It was one o'clock in the morning, but Clodagh was still dressed and fully made-up. She smiled at me whenever she opened the door.

"I was starting to think you weren't coming."

I prided myself on always being on time, but for some reason, I didn't mind being late for her.

"One drink turned into a few, but I'm here now."

She looked like she was holding her disappointment inside, out of fear of my reaction. I never got angry, and I didn't have outbursts, but she probably knew I could walk away more easily than she could. We slept together and then slept together in the other sense. She was a dead body kind of sleeper, thankfully. She didn't bother me with her breathing. Whenever she was awake, she didn't breathe too loudly either. If she had, our relationship would have been very short-lived. By then we'd been together for a couple of months and our friends talked about our relationship in very different ways. From what I'd been told by Greg (the connection between the two circles,) the girls thought it was very cute while the guys thought it was strange that I even had a girlfriend. I thought it was strange I had a girlfriend at all, but she was so pretty to look at and she had so much going for her, whenever she wasn't demanding too much from me. Mostly, it was a fair trade off.

The next morning, I was getting dressed and as always, I was eager to leave. I wanted to get back to my own flat, get a load of laundry done and read some more of my novel. But Clodagh insisted on making me pancakes. I didn't feel like I had the time nor appetite for them, but she was so insistent about it I let her make them. At least I wouldn't have to think about preparing food for a few hours. I waited impatiently in the bedroom. I could hear Clodagh's flatmates banging around in the house and I wasn't in the mood to talk to anyone. I just wanted to sit in silence and listen to some obscure albums. Clodagh had put a record on the turntable. It was spinning around in my head too. She'd listened to the same album on repeat for every visit. It was starting to grate on me. What had at first seemed like an appreciation for good music had become a repetitive and irritating obsession. I tried to tune it out, but I've never been able to do that. I wished I didn't get as angered by sound, but there was nothing I could do about it. It's hard to change your character. I thought it would take ten minutes for Clodagh to make the pancakes, but she was gone for at least half an hour. Whenever she came back, she looked flustered as she handed me the plate.

"They didn't exactly go to plan," she said. "I can't work that gas cooker."

She'd told me she'd always loved cooking and her flatmate had loudly praised her cooking, but the pancakes were horrible. I didn't say anything, and I choked them down out of politeness, but I'd rather have gone hungry. She was obviously embarrassed, and that annoyed me more. Why didn't she just scrap them so we could go to the French café on the corner? At least we knew he could provide something substantial and tasty. As soon as I finished, I lowered my plate to the floor in relief and told her I had to go. She passed me a note, folded up, like a secret-sharing schoolgirl.

"Wait until you leave to open it," she whispered.

I got into the stairwell, and I opened the note. I didn't know what to expect so I didn't have any preconceived feelings about it, but what I read shocked me. "I love you" was written in blue biro. I knew she probably wanted me to run back to the flat, to declare my love for her and to toss aside my plans for the day, but there was no way I was going to do that. The three words made me indescribably uncomfortable. They were like burrs stuck in the surface of my skin. I wanted to tear the note up and release it into the wind, but I knew that would be heartless, so I just put it into my pocket instead and I kept on walking. I got as far away from that situation as I possibly could.

Chapter Twelve

I didn't make the first move to speak to Clodagh after that. I didn't know what to say to her. She had made everything so awkward between us. I didn't know why she'd had to ruin everything with that small piece of paper. After some silence, she asked if I was ok. I responded by suggesting I call over that night. I had some things to do with the band first, and we'd get some drinks in the pub near the studio, but I would spend some time with her after that. I knew I'd be more amenable to it, having had a few drinks. I hoped that would eradicate the embarrassment I felt about seeing her, and the fear that she would bring up the note. I would have been happy to pretend that I'd never seen it. I thought about telling her I'd accidentally dropped it down a drain, but she probably would have rewritten it, perhaps in an even more effusive way. I didn't need to deal with that.

Practice went well and so did a few pints. We had a laugh as a band, and everyone was getting on remarkably well. It's rare that we are all so happy in each other's company. I didn't see my bandmates as a threat because they would never dump love letters on me. We didn't even hug or express our feelings about anything often. We just hung out and played guitar – that was what I was made to do. Whenever I was with them, they might have irritated me, with their sloppy delivery or their silly conflicts, but they never posed the kind of threat to me that Clodagh did.

"Did you read my note?" Clodagh asked, drumming her fingers on her knee with impatience.

"Yeah, I did. I wasn't expecting it."

"Sorry," she said. "I just wanted to tell you. I had to tell you."

There was a long, empty silence, so hollow I could feel it in the pit of my stomach. I had to say something, but I knew there was nothing good to say, other than those three words. So, I gritted my teeth and said them. "I love you too."

Clodagh lit up and she jumped up from the bed, violently hugging me. "I love you," she said. "I was so worried after I gave you that note – that I'd scared you away."

I shook my head unconvincingly.

"I just didn't expect it. I didn't know what to say."

"Yeah, I know. I wanted to tell you to your face, but it was easier to tell you on paper and to do it when you weren't looking at me."

I thought it was a cowardly way to say those three words. I'd never understood them, even in a general sense, but in that situation, I understood them even less. She looked at me, proudly, her cheeks flushed.

"I'm so happy," she continued. "I don't even want to go home for Christmas now. It'll be weird celebrating it without you."

I thought how weird it would have been to celebrate it with her. I'd never been big on Christmas, but the thought of celebrating in his and hers outfits and going to all the traditional events made me feel nauseous. I was relieved she was going home to see her family. It felt like a strange kind of blessing, had I believed in blessings. If blessings were real, we probably would have already made it as a band. But we'd still get there, by hard work rather than luck.

I knew I'd likely have to think ahead to Christmas and consider getting Clodagh a gift. I'd never had to think about that kind of thing before and I had no idea what to get her. I knew she loved vintage things and records and that she had a new interest every week, but it was still time-consuming, thinking of an appropriate present. I knew she'd get me one, because she was so thoughtful, and I knew she was always thinking of me. I was her primary thought, and she was a secondary or tertiary one to me. I knew I could only hide that from her for so long, but for then, it still suited me to have her around. I liked parts of having a girlfriend. She could be very funny and entertaining, whenever she wasn't bringing up the nauseating stuff. She was generous and thoughtful. I liked her physical touch and the attention she gave me after I'd had a few drinks. I liked having somewhere to go at night if I felt like it and she went out of her way to please me. I couldn't contemplate breaking up with her because of our friendship circle either. Her friends were friends with my own. I was starting to see the disadvantage to dating someone with whom you shared mutual friends. If it didn't work out, everyone would think badly of you. Whenever you enter the entire thing, that thought never occurs to you; you're just having fun and not thinking beyond the moment. Maybe, in hindsight, it's better to think of all possible outcomes, and then decide if it's still worth the risk.

It was only November and I felt like Clodagh was arranging Christmas, New Year's and our future wedding without my permission. I felt her grip tightening around me, like I was being strangled. It was a horrible feeling, but I tried not to show it; she'd be really hurt. I didn't feel the need to please her, but I didn't feel the need to purposely hurt her either.

That day, I made a point of going shopping for Clodagh's Christmas present. It was only a couple of weeks until she'd be going back to Ireland to see her family. Then I could breathe for a bit. I walked, aimlessly, around the shops, looking for something I thought would suit her. I got her some candles, a pen, a badge and plenty of chocolate. I didn't want to buy jewellery – partly because I couldn't afford to – partly because it would lead her to believe an engagement ring was coming next. There was no way in hell I would have entertained that idea. It sounded like a type of hell so horrible that those condemned in the afterlife couldn't even have imagined it. I never wanted to get married – whether it was that year or in thirty. I just knew it, like most people know they'll probably never shoot heroin or never commit fraud.

We continued our dating dance – seeing each other late at night, staying together until the morning and then, going our separate ways again. Clodagh had dropped out of her teaching course. I'd thought it was cool that she was going to be an English teacher, so it lessened her appeal a little. She just announced one day that she wasn't going back. She'd come home from her training crying and chain-smoking one day. I hadn't been there, but she'd told me about it. I thought it would blow over, but she officially withdrew from the course. She said it had caused conflict with her dad: he said if she left the course she'd have to come back to Ireland, but she was adamant that she wasn't leaving. She would get a job, but for then, she said I could teach her how to sign on, since I was an expert on that. I didn't know whether to take that as a compliment or an insult.

She went along to her appointment there, worried she wouldn't get any money, but she did. She went to a different benefits office to me, but once you've been to one, you've seen them all. She informed me that she'd received her "getting back to work" book: a little journal we had to fill out as evidence that we were indeed trying to find employment. She seemed to be taking it very seriously. She went home from her meeting and instantly started completing the booklet. She made applications as she went: something that was totally foreign to me.

"If you put down real jobs, you'll get phone calls about them," I said.

I wanted to avoid that at all costs, but Clodagh didn't seem to mind. She told me that she would love to have a job – something to guarantee that she could stay in Glasgow, that she could stay with me. She was interviewing for jobs almost every day, displaying a level of enthusiasm for it that I couldn't understand. Each time I left the job centre with my workbook ticked for another fortnight, I felt like I'd won the lottery. Then, I went home, made myself a cheap fry-up and chain-smoked in bed. I could think of no better celebration.

I didn't understand why Clodagh had left teaching. If she had got into a course that provided such a solid career opportunity, why did she want to walk away? I was worried that she'd turn to me for money too, if she didn't have a career path of her own. I couldn't afford to share with someone else – at least not beyond a coffee and a rollie now and again.

Just as I was starting to worry about that, Clodagh announced that she'd found a job. It was in a gift shop within walking distance of her flat and they wanted her to work every day she could on the run-up to Christmas. She was pleased about the pay, but I could tell she was worried about how little we'd get so see each other. It solved a lot of problems at once for me. If she was working all the time, she couldn't expect more from me all the time. I hoped that meant I would disappoint less, which meant that I'd get what I wanted from her without causing any real damage.

Most unemployed people might be jealous when their partner snaps up a job, but not me. I felt sorry for her, and I was perplexed as to why she was so eager to work. She told me the previous week, she'd been counting out 5p's on the bedroom floor, hoping she had enough for a subway ride, and now she'd have a steady wage coming in. She was delighted. Maybe I'm just better at subsisting on nothing. Some people have fewer needs than others and I am one of them. Life has taught me that, time and again, without fail. I'm different to almost everyone that I meet.

Chapter Thirteen

The band was immensely irritating me. I didn't know how they were so lacking in talent. It felt like they were getting progressively worse with each practice. I was tempted to throw a tantrum and leave. Maybe my upset baby face would make everyone snap out of it and get more work done. They were treating the band like it was just a bit of fun instead of a career choice and their time-wasting was frustrating me. I didn't go for drinks with them after band practice that week, to prove a point, but I didn't know if anyone really noticed they'd annoyed me. It's hard to be so serious about something and have others treat it so cavalierly.

Clodagh was working until close a lot and I went to meet her one day when she was locking up at the shop. It made me feel like I was an official boyfriend though, so I never offered to do it again. She was obviously overjoyed when I met her at the door. She probably thought it was chivalrous of me. I hoped it made a lasting impression, because it would certainly be the last time I did it. I wasn't crazy about being seen out and about in public with her. Thankfully, with the Christmas rush, there was a constant stream of customers, and she was so busy, she barely noticed I wasn't around – or maybe she did, but she didn't have time to lodge a complaint. Sometimes I just thought she wasn't worth the trouble - however special I might have thought she was when we first met.

She was working right up to Christmas and then she was flying home to join her family. She didn't invite me to go with her, and I knew it was because she knew I'd say no. I couldn't think of anything worse than ending up stranded in rural Ireland with the parents of a girl I was half-heartedly dating. I had limited time for her, never mind her family. They'd probably plague me with questions I wouldn't be able to provide satisfactory answers to.

The night I picked Clodagh up from work, we walked back to her flat and ordered a pizza. She hadn't had time to cook – thankfully - so we got *Dominos*. She and her flatmates already had a ceiling-high stack of empty pizza boxes in their hallway, so it didn't matter if we added another one to the collection. It was twenty pounds for a large pizza, and it pained me to pay for it, but Clodagh offered to. She said she had no time now, but she had money. So, I let her get it. It seemed to make her happy, being able to treat me. That night she cuddled close to me and then she fell asleep. Her breathing was loud to my ears. and it felt like she was doing it on purpose to annoy me. Then, the snoring started. I hadn't heard her snore before. I thought someone was either a snorer or they weren't – but she was a secret snorer. I lay wide awake all night, listening to her thick breathing and wishing I was anywhere else in the world.

In the morning, Clodagh nudged me. "What's wrong?"

"You were snoring."

"I'm sorry."

She looked embarrassed, and I was glad she was. It felt fair whenever she'd kept me awake all night. I never would have stayed over had I known she was a snorer. It was like listening to someone gnawing on polystyrene. I couldn't ignore it and I grew angrier by the second as I was forced to listen to it. It was a miracle I hadn't left her in the middle of the night.

I called over to see her once more before she headed home for Christmas, to give her the Christmas presents. As you know, I'd collected a few things that were thoughtful without being costly. She had some presents for me too. None of them were too sentimental. Maybe she was starting to sense that I didn't like that kind of thing. Practical presents were the only kind I liked to receive. She gave me some music related items, a funny teacup and some chocolate. It felt like a fair exchange. I packed up the presents into the plastic bag I'd brought hers in and I took them home. I didn't feel sad about us parting ways for Christmas. It sounded like it was a much bigger deal to her than it was to me.

Chapter Fourteen

The festivities were over quicker than a drummer counting in a punk song. Before I knew it, Clodagh was back on Scottish soil, and she was looking for me. She rarely suggested meeting up. I was grateful she didn't, in a way, but I knew she was waiting for me to do it instead. Her job had come to an end, she said. They said they didn't need extra staff after Christmas, so she was back on the dole until she found a new job.

I called over to her flat a few days after she returned, and we had a fry-up on the sofa. We watched a sitcom in the dark. It was Seinfeld: my choice. She hated it, but she put up with it anyway. I laughed alone. No one had bothered to open the curtains in the living room yet and the Christmas tree was still standing in the corner of the room. It was an over-used artificial thing that one of the girls had borrowed from a family member. It was like a toilet brush with tinsel and baubles on it – I thought, but I've never been a fan of Christmas decorations anyway. Christmas tends to interfere with solitude, unless you have no one to turn to. Families always want to get together and do traditional things. My family aren't as bad as others for that, and I do get along with them reasonably well, but I don't like having too many obligations. I went to my parents' house that Christmas Day. My sister and brother were there too. My brother brought his kids. He has a baby and a toddler. I've never been hugely keen on them. They're always whining and hurting my ears. Thankfully, I don't have to be in their company for too long on Christmas Day, and there is plenty of alcohol at my parents' house, so I can ply myself with that and drown most of it out.

Clodagh was talking about how sad she was that Christmas was over. She said it was her favourite time of the year. I couldn't understand that at all. It felt like all we had in common was music, and the fact our friends were dating, and I'd grown to hate most of her music anyway. It felt like I was biding time, waiting for the right moment to walk away.

"You didn't talk to me much while I was away," said Clodagh, her voice cracking.

"I was just busy."

"I'd like to see more of you."

"I can't meet up any more than we do now."

"Why not?"

"I have the commitment of the band, and I have to have some time to myself too."

Clodagh looked like a chastised puppy, and she was dopily ready to keep trying to show me affection, just like a snubbed puppy does too.

She touched my arm, and I didn't respond to her touch. It felt like bristles on my skin.

"I'm not happy about how little we see each other and how little we talk," she said.

"Sorry, but I don't know what more I can give you."

"In that case, maybe it's time for us to call it a day."

I was shocked she was breaking up with me. I never thought in a million years that she'd do that. I knew she was besotted with me. All it took was one look into her eyes to establish that. She looked at me dreamily and longingly, every time we were together.

"No, please…" I pleaded.

I couldn't stand the thought of us breaking up - on her terms. I was suddenly desperate to hold on to the relationship when I never had been before. Maybe I cared more than I thought I did, I reasoned. Maybe I wasn't good at identifying my feelings, but they were inside me, lying latent – waiting for the right person to activate them.

"We aren't spending enough time together. You never seem to want to see me. What's the point?" she asked me.

"Ok, fine, we can see each other more often," I said. "Let's not break up."

I could see her being won over. She was back on my side again. The dreamy look was returning to her eyes.

"Ok," she smiled, squeezing my hand. "Only if you're sure you want to."

"Yes, we could see each other a couple of times a week – maybe even three times."

She still looked dissatisfied, but she nodded resignedly.

I could probably still get away with keeping our contact to a minimum; I just needed to be a bit more creative with my excuses.

Chapter Fifteen

Clodagh got a new job that week. Her determination to find a job flagged up my reluctance to do so, but I still didn't feel motivated to try. I kept checking in with Fiona at the job centre, getting my sheet ticked and drawing my small fortnightly wage. I had to have free time for the band and for Clodagh. I couldn't have worked a regular job even if the perfect one had been handed to me on a polished platter. There was no such thing as the perfect job anyway.

Although she had passed the interview and been offered the role, Clodagh's job didn't start for another month, so she was just waiting around until then. She talked about it like it was a positive thing; we would have more time together. She had five weeks to spend with me before she was due to start her training week. It felt like an age to me and probably felt too short to her. I had no intention of spending more time with her, but I didn't tell her that. I just nodded and gave her a small smile. She beamed back at me. I could fake it, just to keep that smile there.

The job she'd secured was an impressive one. She'd get to use her English degree on a daily basis. It was a secretarial role, but she'd been hired because of her language skills. They said they needed someone with a flair for writing to compose professional letters and emails for them. She only had to do small administrative tasks whenever she'd completed her assigned work. She'd be paid extra to complete it too. Clodagh was so excited that her degree was finally being put to good use. She'd thought teaching was the end of the road and that she'd be stuck in retail – working happily but without getting to use her subject, but she was pleasantly surprised. I looked forward to her starting work. I couldn't wait for her to be occupied with it. If she was immersed in her work, there was less time left for me.

Over the course of Clodagh's month off, we saw each other a handful of times, mainly late at night, unless we were getting a takeaway from the French café. That was the only reason I would have been happy to go there earlier in the day.

The month passed and Clodagh started her new job. I told her I was excited for her, but really, I was excited for myself. She was working full time hours, Monday to Friday. At the weekend, I knew I'd probably play a gig or two, so that sorted that problem out. Clodagh suggested coming along to our next gig. I didn't mind if she was there; our mutual friends would be anyway, and the gig we were playing was a pretty big deal. We were playing in one of the top music venues in Glasgow. Famous bands had played there before. We'd got in, solely thanks to Jake's persistence. At least his forwardness made up for his lack of talent. I felt inspired and filled with hope again, that the band could still make it. It was a huge leg-up for us. I thought we'd get any gigs we wanted in the city after that. Collectively, we weren't too tight, but I was ready to play single-handedly, had I needed to. I don't often get excited, but I was about that. I wanted Clodagh to be there, in a way – as a mascot, really. It turned out, it felt good to have a cheerleader in the crowd that genuinely believed I was wonderful after all. That was one of the benefits of having a girlfriend. There had to be something that was keeping me there – I supposed it was that and the fact that my friends had stopped talking about me ending up alone forever. They didn't think I was gay or asexual anymore; they just thought I was selfish. I wanted to prove them wrong – that I could have a relationship and it could appear as loving as theirs did, even though I hadn't uttered the three essential words since the day Clodagh had first made me say them.

The gig went smoothly, in my eyes. We sounded our best. Maybe it was the equipment, or maybe it was the pressure of a good, well-paying gig, but everyone pulled out all the stops. If only they could do that every time we were in the studio. I've never thought you should just play well for other people's benefit; you should view it as a matter of pride and do it for yourself. Who wants to sound bad even to themselves? Clodagh seemed really interested at first but after a while, I couldn't see her anymore. I gave up trying to. She must have got talking to her friends or gone to the toilets or something. The fact she wasn't attentively watching us was annoying me. Why had I wasted a ticket on her? How could she come to watch me and then not even bother doing it? Whatever else she was doing could wait until we were finished onstage, as far as I was concerned. She was meant to be my greatest fan, but I hadn't heard her cheer once. Granted, she had a soft voice, and she wasn't really a cheerer, but it still made me feel less important. I finished up on stage and tried to forget about her and not let her blight our gig. We played for a solid thirty minutes and then we made room for the headliners. It was a dub band that bore no resemblance to us in any way. I didn't take that as a bad sign; variety is the spice of life, they say.

I made my way through the crowd. I could see everyone's head since I was taller than most people in the room, but Clodagh didn't appear to even be in the back row. Then, I found Susie. She was crouched on the ground, talking worriedly to Clodagh.

"Oh, Glen, I'm glad you're here - Clodagh fainted."

I didn't know what to say. Why did she have to make a scene at our big gig? She was still on the floor, but she looked fine. A guy was starting to help her to her feet, so I didn't feel like there was anything else I needed to do. I went to join Greg and the others for a post-gig pint. We deserved it after sweating our butts off on stage. Greg was buying, so I put in my order. I'd get the next round. We'd each made fifty quid playing there, so I was better off than I was most weeks. In a way, I wished I could frame the money and display it on the wall – just to mark the importance of the occasion. Once it was spent, it was spent – I knew I might as well use it for something enjoyable, like drinks for the whole band. It was the opportunity we'd had that meant most to me – not the money. Meanwhile, in ranking of importance, Clodagh was sitting below my bottommost afterthoughts.

I didn't see her for the rest of the evening. Eventually, she came to tell me that she was getting a taxi home. I didn't stop her. It was easier to relax when she wasn't there in the background, being let down by me. I knew that was what was happening, every time she looked at me with those big expressive eyes. It didn't matter how carefree she pretended to be; it was always obvious that she was anything but.

I was sure Clodagh's friends were being standoffish with me too, but how did they expect me to rush to her aid mid-gig? I couldn't interrupt a song to jump into the crowd and help her to her feet. She had been in a band herself, so surely, I thought, she'd understand. I buried the whole thing. The next day, I texted her a complimentary message about her hair. She was immediately responsive, so I knew I was still in her good graces. It was ok and the gig didn't get ruined, even though she'd missed most of it. The crowd were decent apart from her. I felt appreciated for who I truly was whenever we were standing on stage, getting applause and cheers. A standing ovation was on my bucket list, but there was still plenty of time to get there. After all, I was only twenty-six.

Chapter Sixteen

It was Valentine's Day – the day I dreaded the most. Clodagh had asked me what I wanted to do for it. I hadn't planned on doing anything. Apart from the fact I didn't have the funds for a meal in a restaurant, the whole thing sounded hellish to me. I didn't even like having to declare my love without any pressure being placed on me, but with a consumerist holiday pushing me to, I wanted to demonstate it even less. I couldn't feel anything at all, in general, so I was lacking whatever I needed to motivate me to make something special of the day.

Clodagh suggested we keep things simple and get the "dine in for two" deal from the shop. You could get two courses and a bottle of wine for a tenner. That sounded much less miserable to me. At least it was oven food, so we could shove it in the oven and forget about it. I wouldn't have to buy it in advance either – I'd have to wait until Valentine's Day to get it. I could dash in and pick it up on my way over. They had a branch of the store not far from Clodagh's flat, so it wouldn't put me out too much. I could think of better ways to spend ten pounds, but it was preferable to anything else she might have suggested. It was just a box-ticking exercise. Have you acknowledged Valentine's Day? Check. Have you arranged something for your partner's benefit? Check. Then it would be over for another year, and we probably wouldn't be together a year from then anyway. That might have sounded cynical, but I had grand plans for my life, and none of them included domesticity.

On Valentine's Day, I slept late. I forgot it was an enforced day of celebration, until I turned on the TV and there was mention of it. It was on the news – as if it was newsworthy. My stomach sank, but my heart didn't move an inch. "Dine in for two" had been my responsibility and I'd forgotten about it. But there was still time to run and grab it before I had to head over to Clodagh's. I told her I was running late but I was on my way. It felt ridiculous that she was waiting for dinner, and I hadn't had breakfast yet, but that's what exhaustion does to a person: your body clock gets confused until it's like you're living in a different time zone to everyone else. You can't be held accountable for your actions.

Whenever I arrived at the shop, it was all but cleared out. I didn't know the" dine in for two" option was so popular. All that remained were some starters and sides. I grabbed a starter, a bottle of juice, since the wine had all been taken, a couple of sides and a dessert. It wasn't an appealing dessert which was why there was such an availability of it. The shelves were stripped of all the good desserts. I paid at the till and hoped that Clodagh would be suitably satisfied with my purchases. I didn't need an evening of earache on top of everything else. I cursed Valentine's Day as I walked to her flat. Why did such a silly celebration have to exist? Whom did it benefit? I passed a few packed restaurants with the diners gazing lovingly into each other's eyes. I gave myself a metaphorical pat on the back for dodging that bullet and kept walking.

I got to Clodagh's about twenty minutes late, but I knew she'd forgive me. She'd forgive me for anything. She had one of those forgiving hearts that can excuse any behaviour, however bad. Punctuality was the least of my worries. She would have forgiven much worse than that. I knew it. You could just read it off her. She was an open book, as they say, but she was even more transparent than that. I could see through her like a window.

When I unpacked what remained of dine in for two, Clodagh was obviously disappointed. I just explained myself and I knew she'd be fine.

"The shelves were empty – I didn't realise it would be so popular."

"It's because it's Valentine's Day," she said.

Her reverence for the festivity disgusted me. Why did we have to celebrate it like everyone else – like all the brainwashed consumers that swarmed around us like dirtied flies?

I proceeded to put everything into the oven, or the microwave where permitted. I poured Clodagh a wine glass of sparkling grape juice. She'd probably be unimpressed that I hadn't got wine, but I could come up with a convincing story.

"I missed the last bottle of wine. There were some pushy people in front of me and I let them go first."

She nodded at me with a look of gentle appreciation, for how polite I was, how self-effacing. She was clueless. I was mildly irritated by the fact that I could have spent the same tenner and got a bottle of wine and some steaks for dinner, but I'd missed out on it. It couldn't be helped. What was done was done, and I'd had a lovely lie-in that morning. My achy body had needed it. It was worth the sacrifice.

We clinked glasses, sitting opposite each other on her balding bedroom carpet.

"Happy Valentine's Day," I said.

I was sparing with the sentiment. It pained me to wish her it. I couldn't stop thinking about how stupid the celebration was: the same thing every year, purely designed to empty wallets whilst convincing the population that they were somehow demonstrating their love in a fitting way.

The meal was underwhelming. It would have been better if we'd just ordered a pizza. I felt like I'd wasted ten pounds on a few scraps I could have fished out of the bin outside the store a few hours later.

When the meal was finished, we had sex. It wasn't passionate; it was robotic. We'd done it the same way the last five times. It felt like a countdown to alone time. I couldn't wait to get out of there, but it would have to wait until the morning. Clodagh wanted to cuddle.

Chapter Seventeen

Clodagh seemed to be enjoying her new job. She was off that weekend, and she made sure to tell me. That was the closest she came to extending an invite to me. She was probably worried I'd turn her down, but her cowardice bothered me. If she really loved me as much as she said she did, why wasn't she more proactive about inviting me over? Granted, I still would have stuck to seeing her on my own terms, but at least I wouldn't have had to arrange the whole thing every single time. At least I wouldn't feel the weight of the guilt she wanted me to feel. I didn't often feel guilty, but knowing she wanted me to was almost the same thing. I offered to stay on the Friday evening, planning on leaving early on Saturday morning to go and play tennis with Greg for a laugh. Neither of us played, and that was why we were going – to laugh at each other, get a bit of exercise and get a drink after. I walked a lot, but there was no reason for my extreme skinniness apart from my fast metabolism. I wasn't a very active person, nor did I put my health first. I chain smoked rollies, ate whenever I felt like it and spent a lot of my time pondering things in bed. I didn't often go out in daylight. I preferred to hibernate in my room. The weather in Glasgow was dire anyway. One day out of a hundred seemed to be sunny, and my skin has never taken to the sun well anyway. I just get pink and freckly and prickly tempered too.

Friday felt far enough away that I was able to enjoy my time alone. I lazed about, playing around on the guitar when the mood struck me and writing down the odd lyric. I devoured another *Murakami* book and drank espresso and smoked myself silly. My flatmates weren't around, so I could take up pride of place in the living room without being disrupted. I was living a bachelor's dream, until I remembered the commitment of my girlfriend and my dread of our upcoming meeting. It couldn't really be called a date. We rarely went out. We rarely left her bed, actually. We just smoked in bed, listening to her music, having sex, sleeping and saying goodbye. If I was lucky, I got fed there. If I was luckier, she didn't make it. There was one meal I could recall eating there that was very good, but I believe she got the recipe from her flatmate. She wasn't exactly culinarily skilled, but she'd just come out of student life, and how many students are? I was too lazy to attend to housework on a regular basis. Now and again, my flatmates and I would come to an agreement about a cleaning rota, but it always went out the window on day two and the espresso cups would start accumulating again – their remaining grounds glued with sugar syrup to the bottom of the cups. A quick rinse sorted out most problems. It didn't really bother me; those weren't the types of things that got on my nerves.

Whenever I got to Clodagh's on Friday, I felt my breathing becoming laboured as I climbed her stairs. The steps to her flat only consisted of one winding flight, but they were large, concrete blocks that tired your feet. I'd made that ascent too many times for my liking. I enjoyed the descent much more, even though I shouldn't have admitted that, even to myself. She let me in, and I followed her into the bedroom. I removed my boots on the edge of the bed, waiting to strip down, do the deed and then have a celebratory smoke. At least the sex was good – whenever I felt like doing it. I didn't have an insatiable need for it, but when it was on offer for free, why not partake in it? It wasn't something you could really take care of yourself – at least not without going to great lengths to do so.

One of my friends went on an annual holiday to Vegas for gambling and to hire a prostitute. I didn't know why he thought it was worth paying for. I would rather have done without it completely than have to spend a penny to get it. Why do that when it was available for free? That was one of the benefits of being a relationship that I could happily acknowledge.

Whenever I got there, I told Clodagh I was leaving early the next morning to play tennis with Greg. She looked unamused as soon as the words left my mouth. I thought it best to give her warning. At least she wouldn't get emotional the moment I left. I hated having to deal with her emotions. Her feelings vacillated so much I could barely keep up. It was hard enough to understand one negative emotion, never mind alternating and entwined positive and negative ones. She was too complex for me and too hard to please. I just wanted to be able to throw her a bit of attention and walk away – like feeding a dog a treat and keeping its affection even whenever you aren't in its sphere. It might pine for you, but whenever you return, it acts like nothing ever happened and you never left in the first place. No such luck with Clodagh.

She was visibly upset, but for once, she said it straight away. "You're going to play tennis in the morning?"

"Yeah, why?"

"I can't believe you're doing that. I've been working all week, and we haven't seen each other once. We finally get to be together and you're leaving to play tennis with a bandmate you've seen all week?"

"We weren't playing tennis then."

"It's not about the tennis."

"It is, kind of."

"No, you never want to see me," she said.

She spat the sentence out like a petulant child. I half-expected her to stick out her bottom lip in a pout and to angrily fold her arms too.

"I'm here now."

"And then you're rushing off as soon as you wake up."

"At least I came."

"Oh, how good of you! It was only for a short time. I thought we were spending the whole weekend together."

I wondered how on earth she could have jumped to that conclusion, especially considering the fact that we had never spent more than twelve hours together, consecutively.

"I'll come over tomorrow night after practice if you want."

"You only ever want to see me at night, and you never want to go anywhere."

"Where would we go?"

"Anywhere."

"I don't have a lot of money."

"You have money for a tennis court."

"Actually, that was a treat from Greg."

"Of course it was," she said, shooting me a look that was like an arrow straight to the eye.

I thought about asking, "what are you trying to say?" but I knew it was just an emotional outburst. And I didn't care enough to react, or to waste time arguing about it – that was the bottom line.

I left, as planned, the next morning. By then, I had talked Clodagh round a bit, and we were still on speaking terms. I promised I'd be back that night, even though it pained me to make such a commitment. I might have wanted to go for a few beers after practice. I was learning first hand why guys complained about their girlfriends and their demands. I'm not the kind to do what someone else wants me to. If I was, I'd have been working a regular job by then. But I guess that was part of what she loved about me: my free spirit and the fact she couldn't tie me down.

I looked at Clodagh. She really was beautiful; she had a face like a doll. Part of me wanted to make her happy, but a bigger part of me didn't feel equipped to do it. I could make frail attempts at it, but I knew her need would always grow in relation to whatever I decided to give her. So, it was probably best for both of us if I gave as little as I could afford to.

Greg and I had a great time playing tennis. Neither of us were natural players, and I knew it would probably be something we did as often as most people played crazy golf, but it was fun for a bit of a diversion on a Saturday morning. I didn't normally see the light of day on a Saturday, or on several other days either. I was sad when the game was over. Time went so much faster whenever no one was demanding anything emotional from me.

As I walked home afterwards, I was sweating profusely and in great need of a shower. It probably didn't help that I was dressed from head to toe in black. I didn't exactly have a wide array of work-out clothes in my wardrobe. I got home and had a long shower. While I was in it, thoughts came to me that I didn't usually make space for. I wondered what I could do to keep Clodagh happy – well, happy-ish. Then, it struck me like fork lightening: she could meet my family. I could take her out somewhere with my folks, and she would feel special, and satisfied enough to stick around for a while, just in case I wanted her to. I wasn't completely committed to her, but I wasn't completely ready to give her up either. I knew she was a catch; I just didn't know that I was the right person to have caught her. She was like a fish that probably needed to be thrown back for another fisherman – one that was looking for a different species than I was. I probably just wanted to see what was in the pool and then put it all back at the end of the fishing session – to let it live and swim freely, without interference from me.

Still, I got ready. I put on the aftershave Clodagh loved and my favourite shirt. We weren't going anywhere, but it was a big night in a way – especially for her. She wouldn't be expecting my invitation at all – I knew that. I knew she felt like there was a huge secretive part of me that she couldn't access. She'd feel like she was gaining access to it – and I was the one offering; she wouldn't be the one pushing for it. Little did she know how little it cost me. My parents might find it unusual seeing me with a girlfriend, but they probably wouldn't give any special meaning to it. They knew I was a lone wolf. They knew what was at the heart of me. It's hard to be brought up by someone and for them to not know that. At least I knew they were discrete. They wouldn't tell her much about me – at least not more than I had already volunteered myself.

I wanted to be the kind of man that Clodagh deserved, but I didn't know if I could ever achieve it. I didn't even know if I was even capable of trying. Some people are just built to have a look at a mess and then walk away whenever others are quick to get their hands dirty. What can I say - I like having clean hands.

Chapter Eighteen

Clodagh was delighted that she was meeting my parents. So delighted, in fact, that I almost felt like I'd done something heroic in giving her permission to meet them. She would accompany us to a football match. My dad wanted to go anyway, so he offered to get us extra tickets. I was partial to football, so I didn't mind going there. At least if we were at a match, there wasn't much of an opportunity for the conversation to get too stilted or for Clodagh to ask them too many questions about me. She was shy whenever she met new people, so I didn't think she would, but I didn't want her to find out anything I didn't want her to know. There was no point in hinting at a level of intimacy that didn't really exist between us, and that never could because of my limitations. I wasn't ashamed of them; they just were what they were. But the average person isn't exactly delighted to learn information like that about their loved one, so I thought it best to keep it quiet.

On the day of the match, Clodagh was obviously excited, which was cute to see, because she loathed sports. The fact she was excited to meet my parents at a football match said a lot about how she felt about me. I was in a good mood too. I met her at the train station next to the stadium. My parents were already waiting outside for us. We walked hand in hand. It really struck me how little we ventured out in public together. It wasn't because I was embarrassed to be seen with Clodagh, physically. She was a true beauty: the kind that regularly invites looks from strangers, irrespective of sexual orientation. It was because I didn't want to be associated with her for other reasons. Her palm was sweaty, and I wanted to let it go, but whenever I tried to drop her hand, she wouldn't let me.

My parents saw me coming and they broke into smiles, walking towards us. They had invited my sister too – it turned out. I'd always got on well with her, but I didn't want her to think the relationship was more serious than it was. She had a boyfriend herself, and she had always nagged me about meeting someone. I didn't want her to get too excited about it or get too involved. She wasn't much older than me, so there was always the potential for her to become good friends with Clodagh. That was dangerous because I didn't need anyone maintaining contact with her should I decide to walk away. I pushed that thought away as everyone started talking and making introductions. They were getting along, it seemed. Clodagh was making a real effort to keep the conversation flowing. It would have made me love her more, had I been capable of that feeling. But I just wanted the match to get started so we could get lost in that and the conversation could be put on hold.

It was a bitterly cold day. It had been snowing and it felt like the chill had hung around even though the snow had mostly melted. It wasn't ideal weather for an outdoor event, but I've never been one for the outdoors anyway. How many musicians are, I wonder? I was wearing a woolly scarf and hat. Clodagh told me I looked cuter whenever I wore a hat – like a cranky baby. She thought that was a compliment, because of my toddler impersonations, but what guy really wants to be compared to a disgruntled baby? Maybe that was part of the reason I wasn't fully invested: she made me feel like I was cute, but I didn't really feel like a man. Had I ever felt like a man? I couldn't answer that question, and I didn't know what would make me feel that way either. Maybe being on stage and making my guitar sing for a besotted crowd.

The match was underwhelming. The team I would have preferred to win lost, but I didn't really care either way. I wasn't passionate about anyone that was playing. I wasn't passionate about anything, apart from my guitar. I was missing it while I was out all day and I looked forward to lying back in bed and playing around on it at the end of the day. One thing was certain: I wouldn't be spending the night at Clodagh's. I found days like that draining, and I knew I'd need alone time afterwards to unwind. By the end of the match, we were all freezing, and my dad suggested grabbing something to eat nearby. They knew a deli that had a dinner menu, so he said we could go there. They'd be paying, so I let them decide what they wanted to do. I would have been happy to call it a day and go home at that point, but my stomach can never turn down a free meal. I like to be looked after; what can I say? Only when I choose it though. I don't like whenever people take it upon themselves to do it without asking first, like Clodagh does.

We went into the deli. It was quite a cramped space and we clustered around a table at the window. Clodagh and I sat closer than I would have liked, but there was no alternative seating choice unless I left the building – and I was the reason everyone was there, so I stuck it out. Clodagh and my dad were talking about music, and she was listing all her musical knowledge. I could tell how hard she was trying to impress him, and I knew she was wasting her time. Even if she did impress him, it didn't really mean anything in the end. They'd likely be strangers one day. I just didn't know when yet. I wanted to keep her around for a while. The positives still outweighed the negatives, overall. There were some minor irritations, but nothing I couldn't deal with to get the attention and sex I wanted. I had to admit, it felt nice to have someone to bring to events. Most of the time, I'd choose my company over anyone else's, but whenever we were in groups, I liked not being the only one there without a date. It was convenient for that. Otherwise, my lone wolf nature would have been much more apparent to everyone I knew. Everyone had stopped asking me when I was going to get myself a girlfriend, and for that, I was grateful.

I could tell that Clodagh thought she was forming a bond with my dad, but I knew better than that. Bonds are almost always broken in the end, for one reason or another. At least I never make them in the first place, so whenever they do break, it doesn't affect me too much. My emotions have always been subdued. That was why I didn't understand Clodagh's outbursts and her fluctuating moods. I was the same way all the time: predictably numb.

Chapter Nineteen

After the big gig, there was nothing else on the horizon. It was becoming maddening, dealing with the band. We got so close to success it was like our fingers were tracing the edges of it, and then they let it go, at the moment of greatest importance. I knew we had to keep working. We needed to up the ante, but they were unwilling. I thought about suggesting getting rid of Jake. I knew we'd sacrifice our friendship along with it, but it was costing the band too much, having him as the singer. He couldn't even carry a basic tune. You could get away with that to a certain extent, if you were trying to emulate bands like The Fall, like we often were, but he was taking it too far. He was off key ninety percent of the time, and the rest of the time, he was just doing spoken word; not songs.

It felt like everything was coming to a head: the band's reconfiguration and my impending break-up with Clodagh. Since her meeting with my parents, I'd felt even less affection for her. Maybe it was because I could see her inserting her claws into my dad, getting too comfortable like an entitled cat. She'd talked about music with him, and I knew, in part, that it was because she genuinely loved it, but the other part made me sick: the part where she was obviously trying to impress him. I didn't think it was working – but she did, and that was bad enough. It felt like she was trying to wheedle her way into the family, wrapping her tendrils around the branches of the family tree. We were tenuously linked as it was. I didn't need someone trying to strengthen bonds that had been happily distant for years. I liked the way things were with my family. We popped in and out, eating dinner together, discussing light topics and then returning to our respective lives. They didn't ask too much of me or interrogate me about my private life. I didn't need the upheaval of bringing someone new into the family that had the power to change that dynamic. Clodagh would have to go.

On top of that, I had stayed at hers one night since the meeting and she had behaved reprehensibly. We were awoken by the Saturday sounds of the café downstairs: the typical tantrums that transpired each time another parent attempted to have brunch in a civilised manner with a three-year-old in tow. Kids - I still couldn't stand them. Clodagh would coo over how cute they sounded – granted, she acknowledged the annoyance of being woken by spoilt behaviour at nine at the weekend, but she still seemed taken in by them, and able to laugh it off. She was probably the type that would push for kids a couple of years from then, and for an engagement, or even just a more substantial commitment – all of which I was unwilling to give her. Prettiness can cover up certain annoying characteristics, for a while. But her prettiness was becoming dull to me. I'd been looking at it for seven months and the novelty was wearing off.

After that, Clodagh had suggested we get up and go out for breakfast ourselves or do something in a public space. I refused to do that. I was too groggy, and I wanted to sleep until eleven, at least. I didn't particularly want to go out with her in daylight either. If I did, I ran the risk of bumping into someone I knew and having to explain my connection to Clodagh: the one I was planning to soon sever. Clodagh got upset, but instead of discussing it like an adult, she huffily got out of bed, dressed herself like she was angry with her clothes and then stormed out of the flat. I knew a better man would have followed her, but honestly, I was just relieved I had the peace I'd been craving. I fell asleep again and slept soundly until eleven, as planned.

A couple of hours later, Clodagh eventually returned. She was in foul form. I could feel it without even looking at her face. Her anger was carrying on the air waves. I didn't want to risk further incitement, so I avoided the subject.

"Did you do anything nice?"

"I just went for a long walk and thought about things."

"Where did you go?"

"I went to the Botanic Gardens and walked around a book fair they were holding there. I looked in the palm house too. Then, I didn't know what else to do, so I went for coffee and read my book."

"Do you feel better?" I asked.

I was so afraid to ask it that I felt like a secret agent ducking below the parapet, waiting for ensuing gunfire.

"I guess," she said, shortly.

"Sorry I have to go," I said, dressing myself in a hurry after my languid morning beneath her bedsheets.

"Yeah," she trailed off, gazing out the window.

She looked lost and desperate for comfort, but I couldn't give it to her. I knew it was best that I didn't offer more than I was able to give. There was no point in encouraging her dependency on me. It had already formed by its own volition; I could see that, but I didn't need to do anything to strengthen it. I knew the moment for the break-up had come, but she was too fragile – too unpredictable. I promised myself I'd tackle it next time, for my own sake. Once I cut myself free from her, I knew I'd feel a million times lighter.

Chapter Twenty

At practice, the songs were a sloppy mess, but I didn't say anything. We had problems without me creating more – or at least without me bringing the already existent ones to the fore. Stevie the drummer had announced his departure. It had taken us all by surprise. I didn't want to lose him. He was technically alright, and he was good at timekeeping. He kept us together whenever we were completely falling apart. It felt like the ultimate betrayal. He'd left us in the lurch, and I had no idea who we'd get to replace him. Jake had already arranged a few auditions. Why did he have to be the people person? If we didn't have him, I knew we'd struggle to get gigs, talk to the audience, line up our own auditions. He was proactive. I was just a shame that he couldn't sing; more than that - it was a disgrace.

With our drummer gone, we couldn't afford to lose him. The auditions were tedious. We listened to many guys banging out what they thought was a great beat on the kit, but none of it was. I didn't care about how much flair they showed whenever they were playing fills. If they couldn't keep a straight beat, it meant nothing. I wanted session musicians – that was the level of skill I was looking for. But we just kept encountering substandard musicianship. It was like a curse. I knew that it didn't help that our singer wasn't great. What great musicians want to play in a band with a bad singer? It's like they're demeaning themselves or thinking that they can't do any better. It's like people that stay safe their whole lives, too scared to take a risk but depriving themselves of so much opportunity because of it. It's like that saying, "jump and the net will appear," except it's hard to do that whenever it involves friendship. I don't want to mess up our friendship circle, so I always go in a circle and come back to the same point again.

Maybe it'll become incumbent upon me to leave the band. Maybe that's how the net will appear: I won't find a better band until I leave this one. Maybe that's why our drummer left: he saw the musical mess we were in, and he didn't want to waste his talents any longer. If it hadn't been for that gig in Tut's, I didn't think we'd ever make anything of ourselves either. But I always come back to the "what ifs?" What if I leave and the next week they announce their biggest gig yet? Or what if I leave and they set off on tour around England? Going to London with the band is my dream, but would it be as rewarding doing it with people that weren't already your friends? At least we know we get along well, if we're going to have to spend a lot of time together in a confined space. Even at that, I'm sure we would need to partake in substances to make it bearable. I've never had to share a bedroom with someone in my life, at least not for more than a sleepover. I've always had a cave of my own to escape to.

Thinking about the band and how tied I was to it made me angry. I'd talked about it truthfully with Clodagh before. I knew I could because she thought Jake was a terrible singer too, and we could laugh at his singing together, knowing that neither of us would repeat the conversation. She cared about me too much to break my trust – even if we broke up. At least I knew I was safe in that way – no matter what I did to her.

The next day was the day to offload Clodagh. I was tired of dodging that particular bullet. I couldn't pretend anymore. For a while, it had been gratifying having sex with Clodagh, but now it was a chore. Most of the time, I didn't want to, and she repeatedly asked me what was wrong whenever I didn't touch her. I didn't want to lie and cuddle, or kiss, or anything more than that. I had developed a special feeling of disgust reserved only for her. It must have been because we were romantically involved, and I resented her, for always wanting more from me. My friends never demanded much from me, nor did my family. The moment had come for me to be honest with her: I wanted out. I messaged and told her I was coming over, assuming she was in, of course. She always was at that time, unless she was working. She told me to come straight over. I could sense her anticipation, and some cruel part of me couldn't wait to burst her bubble of excitement. I didn't know why I felt that way, but I did. Her presence was annoying me. She'd become like a wasp to me. Her life was worth little, and I just wanted to swat her away every time she came at me. And she continued to come at me, with the same level of persistence as a raging hornet.

She accepted my invitation quicker than I could have typed a message and I set off for the subway. I didn't plan to stay long. If I made it quick, I could get home before the last subway and relax. I knew the feeling would be sweet once it was done, but dread was overcoming me. I could picture the look on her face whenever I made our break-up final. She had tried to break up with me not long before that, because I hadn't rushed to tell her I loved her. I wished I'd just accepted it then, and not tried to keep it going, thinking there was more I could get out of it. It was so much hassle for very little return. It had been like fanning a fire that was already extinguished.

Clodagh buzzed me in, and we went straight to her bedroom, as always. She closed the door, and I sat on the edge of the bed, waiting for her to join me.

"You look so serious," she said. "Where's the grumpy toddler?" she laughed.

I didn't laugh. I didn't find it funny anymore. It had ceased to be funny after the first time we had joked about it, and she was just wearing it out now – wringing it out like a towel without a drop of water left in it.

She didn't sit down. Instead, she stood, waiting for my face to break into a smile. Her disappointment was palpable, and it gave me an ugly feeling. I wanted to run away from it, to never have to look into her distressed eyes again. She was over-emotional, and probably was in every area of her life. That wasn't my fault, and I wanted to be free of it. I couldn't stand to look into those sorrowful eyes for another second. It was time to take off the tourniquet, no matter how bad the bleeding was after it.

"I think we should break up," I said, tentatively.

"What? Why?"

"I just don't want this."

"What'd I do?"

"Nothing, specifically. I just can't make myself want this."

"But I love you."

"I know, I'm sorry. I don't think I can feel love."

"You said you loved me."

"I'm sorry."

"Can we try harder?"

"I already tried. I'm sorry – I just can't do it anymore."

"What's wrong with me?"

"Nothing."

"There must be something seriously wrong with me if this is happening."

"Some things just don't work out – it's not anybody's fault."

"But if I'd done the right things, you wouldn't want to leave."

"I tried, I'm sorry."

"So, I tried to break up with you and you wouldn't let me and now you're breaking up with me?"

"I'm sorry."

"You keep saying that, but it doesn't mean anything."

"What else can I say?"

"That you'll stay – that you love me. I don't know how I'm going to manage everything without you."

She was taking it even harder than I'd anticipated. I couldn't stand the crushing disappointment I felt coming from her. It was like I was between the claws of one of those rubbish crushers, about to get the life squeezed out of me.

"How will I get through life without the grumpy toddler?" she said.

I knew she was trying to pluck on my heartstrings. The problem was, she thought there was an internal harp that had never been there. Nothing could pull on my heartstrings, because they'd never existed in the first place.

"I'm going to throw up," she said, racing out the door.

I followed her into the hall, but she'd already barricaded herself in the bathroom. I couldn't hear any wretching sounds, so I hoped she was just being dramatic. She'd probably be fine after I left. I was just being honest with her, and nothing bad could come from being honest – could it?

Her flatmates and their boyfriends were congregated in the tiny kitchen. They were standing around, laughing and smoking, oblivious of everything that was happening in the room next door.

"Glen!" someone called.

They'd noticed me before I had a chance to remove myself. I gave them a sheepish smile and joined them in the already overcrowded kitchen. They were in great spirits, and it conflicted with my own. I didn't know what to say, so I just shared the truth.

"Clodagh is sick. I broke up with her and she's in the bathroom now, throwing up."

"Maybe you should go home now," said Susie.

"No, I should make sure she's ok."

"That isn't really your responsibility anymore."

"Still, I don't want to be a dick."

I said it, but I knew Clodagh would probably think of me as one, no matter what I said. Or maybe she'd just blame the whole thing on herself. She had a tendency to turn everything inward and punish herself for external events that had little to do with her. Our demise wasn't really her doing; she might have precipitated it in a way, but it had always been inevitable. I lacked something basic that you needed, in order to sustain a relationship.

A few minutes later, Clodagh emerged from the bathroom, looking worse than when she'd entered. She was deathly pale and silent. She ignored me and padded along the hall in her socks – the opposite to storming off, but just as pointed. I followed her into the bedroom. I wanted to help her, but it's hard to help the person you're hurting. She was lying on her bed, facing the wall.

"What's wrong with me?" she asked the atmosphere.

It didn't feel like a question I was qualified to answer. I must have thought there was something wrong with her, or I would have wanted to be with her – or maybe I was the one that had something wrong with me. Maybe if I impressed that on her, she'd feel better.

"There is nothing wrong with you. You're fun, and funny and caring. It's me."

"None of that is true. If it was, you'd want to be with me."

"I'm a lot colder than you think I am."

She looked into my eyes, and I could tell from her love-filled gaze that she would always think of me as the funny, cuddly, grumpy toddler. She'd never understand why I dumped her, and she'd never naturally let it go. We could have lain in her bed forever, just going over the whys of the entire situation. I lit her a cigarette and popped it into her mouth. I offered her the ring on my finger – the one that I'd got abroad and never seen anything similar to since. She refused it.

"But you love it," I said, pleadingly.

It felt like my get of jail free card. I liked the thing, but if giving it up meant I could get out of there sooner, I could easily part with the ring.

"No, just keep it," she said. "I want you to have it."

"I want you to have it," I said.

"But it isn't the same as having you."

She was crying hysterically by that stage. Every one of her sentences was hard to make out. All the strength and individuality that had initially drawn me to her was nowhere to be seen.

"I'm going to go," I said, getting to my feet and pulling my jacket on. "I'm just making things worse."

I wanted to get out of there immediately. I had to lace up my boots too. I worked quickly, whilst trying to make it look like I wasn't hurrying. Once I walked out that door, I'd be a free man again. I'd had seven long months of not having that feeling.

As I walked to the door, I heard Clodagh get off the bed. It made a thump, like whenever a cat jumps down. She was moving towards the window. She pushed it up and proceeded to throw herself out of it. I threw myself across the room and grabbed her by the ankles, pulling her with all the force I had in me. She fell to the bedroom floor. It was preferable to the alternative. We were only on the first floor, but there was a huge drop between the tall tenement window and the concrete, especially when you were going head-first. She lay on the floor, and I sat beside her, trembling. Just because I didn't care about her as I should have, it didn't mean I could cope with seeing her trying to take her own life.

I sat still, glued to the carpet with sheer shock. I still wanted to leave, but I couldn't risk something happening to her. I couldn't be the cause of someone's death. There were things even I couldn't forgive myself for. Clodagh was basically good too – reactive - but a good person.

"If I didn't stop you, would you have jumped the whole way?" I asked.

She nodded quietly but affirmatively. I wanted to leave even more than before.

I tucked her into bed, like she was a child. Emotionally, she probably was. Then I left. She begged me to stay, but I quietly refused. I didn't want to be swept up into her problems. That was one of the benefits of breaking up with someone: you could walk away from their drama, allegedly unscathed. I shut the door carefully and respectfully behind me and let myself out of the flat. I knew I'd never set foot in the place again. I'd miss the French guy's café on the corner and the cheap baccy next door. I'd miss the handiness of the subway too. I'd miss the conveniences of it all, but I wouldn't miss the emotional ties and the feeling of obligation that came from Clodagh. I was more than ready to say goodbye. I didn't even turn back for a last look at her window. She'd be ok in there, I told myself. At least now that I'd left the building, it was out of my hands. I was on to better things, all by myself – just the way I liked it.

Chapter Twenty-One

Later that week, whenever I was enjoying my first taste of freedom, I got a phone call from Susie. She said that she had just left the hospital with Clodagh. Clodagh had taken an overdose, but Susie insisted that she was fine. I had no intention of going there, even if she wasn't ok. My link to her was broken. It felt so far in the past that I barely remembered it by then. I was busy with the band and with reading my way through all my *Murakami* novels, drinking espresso and sleeping until four pm. Being single was even sweeter than I'd remembered. There was no way I was reverting to our original arrangement. Susie assured me that Clodagh would be ok. She'd taken the day off work to look after her. I didn't know why she'd bothered to phone me, but then she told me why: Clodagh had asked her to. Why couldn't she release me from her vice-like grip? What did she expect me to do? Grow a heart and make room in it for her?

Clodagh had her own life in Glasgow, and gladly, the city was big enough that we could both live there and never run into each other again. I thanked fate for not placing her in the south side of Glasgow, right on my doorstep. That would have been horrendous. She probably would have hung around on my street corner, waiting for me to emerge from my building, just so she could do her best puppy eyes at me. I wouldn't have put stalking past her by that stage. She was obviously completely obsessed with me: obsessed and unhinged.

I sank my teeth into songwriting. They say the best songs come from heartache, but I couldn't feel any. I wrote about other things instead: the nature of time, the darkness in the city, stories other people had told me. I couldn't really draw on my own experiences because I didn't feel like I'd had that many. I'd spent a lot of my life alone in my room, composing songs about things I hadn't experienced firsthand. Clodagh thought I was deep like she was, but really, there wasn't much beneath the surface. I didn't want her to know that, or anyone else. It's not exactly something you want to advertise about yourself.

The band planned to go on tour over the summer. We didn't know the logistics of it all, but we had a shared dream in mind. We would get a van, drive from place to place and play as many gigs as we could get. We'd have to get copies of our CD's made in advance of it. We could get some merchandise made, but I knew I'd end up designing it too. I always had to pick up the slack.

Whenever I got home at the end of the day, I found some emails in my inbox from Clodagh. The subject line should have been warning enough, but I somehow felt compelled to open them and read their contents. It was mostly nonsensical, hysterical stuff. None of it surprised me. She alternated between blaming me for our break-up and apologising for everything she'd done, begging me to reconsider. I deleted each one without replying. Once they were deleted, I could pretend they had never existed.

It felt like she was trying to haunt me, even though she was still around. I couldn't have let her fall from the window, no matter how much she bothered me. I'd saved her life, but I couldn't feel proud of it. I knew she needed help, in the professional meaning of the word. I couldn't have done anything more to help anyway.

Finally, after being bombarded with messages and emails of desperation, I replied with the words "please get help." She didn't respond. It seemed that those were the three magic words that made her disappear.

Chapter   Twenty-Two

It was a new chapter of my life, and I was excited about the future. I could fly solo with nothing shackling me. I was never made for that kind of united existence anyway. If I felt the need for human company, my bandmates and my sister filled the void. I didn't need anything more than that, and I never had.

Greg told me that he'd bumped into Susie at a party. She'd reported that Clodagh was doing well; she was enjoying making jewellery and being creative. She'd survived the break-up, it seemed – on the surface at least. I doubted that it could be going that smoothly for her, but I didn't wish to hear updates either. Why do people feel the need to provide updates on your ex-partner? If you wanted to know what was going on with them, you would have remained in contact. If you truly cared about them, you wouldn't have broken up in the first place.

I strove to forget her name and I moved on with my life. The band and I were going on a summer tour. Jake had set it all up. My sister invited me over to hers for dinner before we left. She said she'd make a sausage casserole and we could watch sitcoms and catch up. She didn't smoke, so I'd have to go outside for a cig, which was off-putting, but other than that, we got along well. I just hoped she wouldn't nag me about my relationship ending. She had no idea how happy I was that it had, and if I told her, she'd think I had serious problems.

Whenever I went to Jill's house, she was visibly excited to see me. She embraced me and I didn't stop her. I liked seeing her happy and she'd always been so affable and cheerful with me. She started to talk about her own jewellery making, and I felt a bit sick to my stomach. Why did Clodagh have to make her mark on everything to the point that I couldn't associate it with anyone else?

We still had a pleasant evening, and thankfully she didn't mention much about Clodagh. She already knew we'd broken up and she hadn't shared any thoughts when she'd met her, other than saying she was "nice." We weren't so involved in each other's lives that my life decisions really affected her.

After we had dinner, I headed home before the subway closed. I was making plans in my mind for the summer. It was going to be spectacular, and I was ready to get out of Glasgow for a while. It was time to branch out and make ourselves known beyond the bounds of the city.

Whenever I left Jill's that night, I thought about the fact that it had been enjoyable seeing her, but still, I wouldn't pine for her if I didn't see her for years. I wondered if that was normal, and I supposed that it probably wasn't. But how can you decide whether something is normal if you've never known a different way of being? If it doesn't cause you any personal trouble or grief, is it even a problem?

Chapter Twenty-Three

The bus was set up and we were ready to go. It was July and the weather didn't promise to be good, but we were mostly playing at indoor venues, so it didn't matter. I would have happily played in a hurricane if it meant we got to play in public. I was finally moving towards my life's purpose. I'd stopped wasting time with the wrong people, sitting around in Glasgow, wishing things were different.

There were five of us on the minibus. Kyle was driving. He was a guy that hung around with us and called himself our manager, but I wasn't sure who had assigned him that role. For once, he had proven useful to us, since none of the rest of us could drive. We hadn't thought through how we'd survive on the bus for two months together, but it would all fall into place, so long as we got to play gigs. I'd always hated the feeling that came whenever a gig ended. I didn't like the vast nothingness that followed, where you'd sit around wondering when your next gig would come along. This was a dream to me: knowing we'd play every single night for two months. I didn't care how tired I got or how sore my fingers got. It was the closest feeling I'd ever felt to love: the connection I had to my guitar.

Gig one was in in Newcastle. It wasn't a place I'd ever been to before. The only venturing below the border I'd done was a single trip I'd made to London with my family. This was a completely different look at England. I'd always seen it as a less hospitable environment than Scotland, but I hadn't approached it from a gigging perspective. I felt excited. I never got excited about anything, to the point that I didn't understand others' excitement. It just seemed like an unnecessary emotion – one that led people into places they didn't need to be in. Take Clodagh, for instance – had she not been like an over-excited puppy, we never would have established that initial contact. I never would have made the first move. But Clodagh needed to be forgotten. Whatever feelings of discomfort she brought up were irrelevant to my life then, and I hoped she didn't know about our tour of England.

Whenever I broke up with her, she'd suggested packing in her life in Glasgow and returning to Ireland. I'd told her not to, limply telling her she had a life there that went far beyond me. She had a job and friends and her apartment. Why would she leave and start over back home just because of a trivial breakup? Gladly, she wasn't my concern anymore. If she decided to "off" herself, it wasn't my fault, nor was it my responsibility to talk her off the ledge. She'd scarred me for life with that pathetic window incident, and part of me hated her for it – for dragging me into her drama and making me play the role of the hero, when I hadn't put myself forward for it. That wasn't who I was; I'd spent my life running away from other people's problems. I didn't want to be touched by them.

I wished I could shake all memory of her from my mind. I was moving towards a brighter future without the worry of whether I was letting anyone down. I was living for me – and me alone. I might have been part of a band, but in the end of the day, no one was emotionally dependent on me. We were just friends that drank and jammed together. That kind of bond meant more to me than anything "deeper" ever could.

I didn't know what to expect from our first gig. I thought we'd get a distracted crowd, like what we were used to in Glasgow. When you play a smaller gig, unless you've invited enough friends to get the crowd going, it tends to fall flat. People are more interested in their drinks than they are in the performance they're watching. It's just background noise to their other activities. But this was completely different. We didn't walk onstage to the sound of our band name being chanted throughout the venue, but we had an attentive audience, waiting for every note we played. They were receptive to us, and they behaved how I'd always hoped a crowd would. They danced when we wanted them to, and they looked pensive when we wanted them to. It was more rewarding than I could have imagined. I was instantly hooked. I didn't want to put down roots again. I wanted to spend my life in perpetual motion, travelling from place to place. Some people never adjust to that lifestyle, I've been told. It most definitely isn't for everyone, but I must have been the type of person that was perfectly suited to it. I finally felt at home. I'd never felt sad I lacked one – just misplaced. It was like I'd been dropped from the sky and landed in lots of different scenarios – none of which I was comfortable in. But this was the complete converse to that. I felt like I'd finally returned to my homebase, after the most excruciatingly long stopover in a place that bored me.

I played my guitar with the energy most people put into love making. I've never entirely understood it. It didn't leave me with a good feeling, but getting a beautiful sound to issue from my guitar ignited my passion. I trusted it and I knew it's body better than I'd ever known a human form. I wanted to know the intricacies of it, and I was always happy to learn a new detail I had previously missed – however small.

The crowd were warm and welcoming. They listened intently to every bar. It was the best feeling in the world – hearing songs I had written with my own ear and my own words, amplified throughout the entire venue, with people appreciatively swaying to the sound of it. It must have been how people felt whenever they witnessed the birth of their child, seeing their own features in the baby's face and hearing everyone gushing about how incredible it was. I'd never know that feeling, but the one I was discovering was a million times better to me.

It was funny because I'd never thought of myself as someone that stood out. I kept my voice down and I didn't push my way to the front of the stage. I didn't take up more than the allocated area for my feet and my amp. I had red hair and pasty skin, a forgettable face and a spindly figure, but I felt like I owned that stage that night. It was the beginning of an obsession that I could pursue for the rest of my life, and my fix could be found in another gig.

After the show, we hung around and talked to some of the crowd. They were mostly from Newcastle and the surrounding area, but we met a few Scots there. They praised our performance. It was the best one we'd ever had. The energy in the room was unmatched. I could feel it flowing around us long after we'd finished playing. A lady approached me, and I could tell she was flirting with me. She caressed my arm and gazed into my eyes, talking about the uniqueness of our songs and asking for our life stories, summed up in a few sentences. She might have thought she'd get somewhere with me. She probably thought I had that homely look that meant that I'd be a nice boy to bring home to meet Mummy and Daddy, whenever she could tear me away from touring, at least. But she'd be wasting her time, and I was thankful that we were moving on the next day. It would be my way of evading the hangers-on that didn't know how to take a hint, and I could keep up the pretence of being pleasant for a couple of hours. If I could almost manage it for seven months, I could do it for one night.

I was buzzing - as were my bandmates. I could hear bits and pieces of the conversations they were swirling around us and I knew it was a feeling we were all experiencing, that would bind us together for life, whatever happened next. Even if Greg had heard stories from Susie that made him think I was an uncaring, unfeeling jerk, he'd forget them. It would be overwritten by the night we were having. He got me a pint and I took it gratefully. It was gorgeously cool in my hand, my fingers traced lines through the condensation. I knocked it back. It was the most refreshing pint I've ever tasted. After years of hard work, I really had earned it.

That night, we all crammed back into our tour bus. It was more like a minivan, but we didn't care. I would have slept in an upright coffin, like a vampire for life if it meant I got to continue my dream of touring. The material of my dreams was playing out in real life. How many people could say that – even if they had a heart? Maybe I did have one buried somewhere, but my affections were unconventional, so I was classed as a cold being. I had done it myself, but I was still learning who I was. At the age of twenty-six, can many of us be held responsible for our actions? We're still testing the waters of adulthood. But people hold on to grudges, and I knew that Clodagh would. I would have preferred if we had parted on a positive note, but there was nothing I could or would do to improve that.

We got drunk and then we passed out in the van, criss-crossing our feet over each other's since there was so little room to sleep. We had to prioritise our equipment. If it didn't fit, we would have had to get out and walk. We were nothing without our effects pedals – we were one of those synthesiser-type of bands. An unplugged version wouldn't have had the same effect, so we had to have our priorities straight.

The next night was in another city. We had a gig lined up in Durham and I was dying to get started. Our friends from the previous evening had all dispersed and gone home, or back to wherever they were staying. Some had only been there for the headliners, but they still showed us respect and appreciation. It didn't seem to matter that Jake sounded like shit. He could get the crowd excited, and that was all we needed. I did my best to keep him in tune with my backing vocals, but I'm sure the guy is tone deaf. I kept telling myself that maybe tone deafness didn't matter with our kind of music, that it might even prove beneficial.

We didn't see much of the cities we'd passed through. We slept in daylight. That, combined with the fact that the windows on the van were blacked out for the sake of privacy, we didn't exactly enjoy the view. But the scenery didn't matter. We could have been playing in a war-ravaged country and I wouldn't have minded, as long as I got to plug in my amp and make my music.

Durham was calmer. It had a different vibe to it. It wasn't disappointing or inferior to the previous night; it was just quieter. The change of pace and tone was interesting, and it felt like we were playing a completely different gig, even though the setlist was set in stone for the duration of the tour. We weren't going to deviate from it. Our singer didn't have enough prowess to handle those kinds of changes. I put all of myself into the delivery of our songs. I would say my soul, but I'm not sure I have one of those. I don't know if I believe that anyone does. I'm a lot more fatalistic than that. I think we're born, we die, and we're gone. We might do plenty of fun and fulfilling things in between, but they're all as fleeting as the petals on a flower.

I played the entire gig pitch perfect. I didn't make one mistake on my guitar. With the heat of the stage lights and the inevitable sweat, that was an achievement. I felt married to my guitar whenever we stood together in public. I was proud to be seen with her. I know it's a bit outdated for people to feminise objects, but I've always felt like my guitar had female energy. Maybe that is enough to satiate my desires.

We rounded off the gig with an encore and a few extra songs, to surprise the listeners. We were getting paid one hundred a piece for the gig, so we wanted to make sure our customers were satisfied and that they kept coming back for more.

After the gig, we went backstage, where we could drink in peace and talk to each other. I didn't feel like making small talk with people that would be our friends for one night and then, tomorrow, strangers again. I wanted the predictable comfort of my circle of friends that I had kept for years. Greg might have had empathy for Clodagh – thanks to his relationship with his own girlfriend and their mutual friend connection, but I knew he'd always have something deeper for me. That's the kind of thing that only time and long chats over music can produce. He'd remain on my side, no matter what anyone said - no matter what he knew about me.

We hadn't discussed the break-up yet. Maybe he thought I wanted it to remain private – but more likely than that, we had a code between us that said we avoided uncomfortable topics unless completely necessary – or unless we were completely drunk. I'd never asked anything personal about his relationship with Deborah. I didn't understand what he'd managed to see in her for five years. For such a young guy, he'd devoted a lot of his time to her. She was a smiley, friendly type of girl, but there was nothing remarkable about her. At least with Clodagh, I'd seen something different in her – something that aroused my curiosity for a short time. I couldn't begin to understand the inner workings of a conventional relationship – or one that hadn't been constructed upon music alone.

That was all I really had – music alone.

Chapter Twenty-Four

We had a night off gigging, so we decided to explore Durham a bit before we headed to the next city. It was a quaint, steeple topped kind of place. There was something about it that reminded me of the university area of Glasgow. I had positive associations with Glasgow, but I felt a bit haunted by the West End. It was the area where all the drama had ensued. Even though I'd had many other reasons to go to the place over the years, it felt like that would be the most lasting impression I had of it. But I caught myself as I had that thought. I was allowing my thoughts to drift to Clodagh again. Anyone that could have heard my thoughts would have thought that I was attached to her. It wasn't that, but her actions stayed with me. It's hard to separate yourself from something as shocking as that, no matter how hard you try to. I've never struggled to separate myself from anything before, so it's a strange sensation. People always talk about how their senses bring up memories for them. I had never experienced that before, but sights and sounds were reminding me of the night I had forbidden from my thoughts. Being busy with the band was essential for my survival. A day off was too much to deal with. I found myself endlessly worrying about every eventuality that might happen, and I have never been a worrier. But maybe one incident can spark a strange reaction in anyone, if it's shocking enough.

We walked the medieval streets, visiting the cathedral and stopping in cafes, spending the cash we'd made the previous night, but saving most of it. We didn't take our earnings lightly. It felt so good, earning a substantial wage just for playing music. Part of me wanted to get the banknotes framed instead of frivolously wasting them on coffee and sandwiches. We had limited resources in our van, so we had to eat out, even if we didn't want to. Thankfully, at that time, you could still get a sub of the day for two pounds. We could sustain ourselves on *Subway* alone if we had to. It was pleasant walking around a new city, uncovering its sights, and I knew that even *The Cure* would have taken days out to walk around. But I was there for the music, not for the sights. I couldn't wait to get back on the stage. I had new songs I wanted to incorporate into our set list, but I knew we were safest sticking to the standards, with Jake's limitations. We could practise the new songs when we got back to Glasgow, if we ever did. If someone agreed to host us every night of the year, I would have played 365 gigs in a row without ever feeling the need for a break or to return home. What tied me to my home city, really? I might have had a basically functional family, but we didn't see each other every day. The band was my family, irritations and all, and it felt like we were finally going to make it. You hope if you work hard every day, your efforts will eventually pay off. You hope that your fanciful delusions will become reality, and mine were. You don't have to deserve or earn success; it just finds you whenever you're working hard and keeping focused on your goal. I knew Clodagh wouldn't have been happy with my touring. She couldn't even be happy when I put a friend before her for the night. She couldn't have coped with the extended trips away, so I was happy I had burnt bridges with her before setting off. The last thing I needed were tearful phone calls and pleas to hurry home whenever I was doing the only thing I cared about in the world.

We headed to Middlesborough after that. The day spent in Durham had given me too much headspace, and I wanted to disappear into the music again. I was making a concerted effort to keep Clodagh out of my thoughts. She had a tendency to slip into them, like she tiptoed in through a side door when you were unguarded. But I knew it was just because of the ordeal we'd been through; it wasn't because of any longing I felt for her.

The next gig was great. It was our best yet. Maybe a night off had been the medicine the band needed. Word was spreading of our performances in Newcastle and Durham, and more fans were turning up. I guess that's how you build a following: people talk about what they've enjoyed and make other people curious. Or they become obsessed with you and start stalking you, following you, like Clodagh. I wouldn't put that past her. I caught myself thinking about her again.

I thought about my guitar tone. It was perfection. I couldn't wait to plug in the cable and start running scales. I needed to warm up my fingers. They were cold from standing in the night air, smoking cigarette after cigarette. I was still smoking my rollies. I probably always would, even if I was a millionaire. I hoped that was still a possibility. Maybe we would gain recognition, just by showing up every night and putting in the work. Some bands are overnight sensations, but others come from toil and determination. How many post-punk bands have you heard of that have blown up overnight? It's more of a tempered kind of music that builds towards a grand crescendo.

At the gig, we got warmed up. The crowd were already stampeding the stage, ready for the night's entertainment. They'd had a lot to drink; you could tell by watching the swaying sea of faces. Everybody was pressed up against each other, getting over-friendly for so short an interaction. I could feel their impatience mounting as we got tuned up. They would probably go nuts as soon as we played a recognisable chord. It was hard to predict the kind of crowd you'd get, I realised. You might think you'd get the most recognition in a big-name city, but it might be in the smaller boroughs that you found your true fans.

I played with a passion lacking from everything else I did in my life. It was like I was making love to the audience, through the medium of my guitar. They were cheering and chanting, singing along with lyrics they made up as they went along. It was worth all the work. I couldn't wait until the night arrived when the crowd could sing every song word for word and get them right.

Greg and the others looked happy too, but not to the same extent as me. I was riding on a wave of ecstasy. It was strange, because I'd always been the one that lacked emotion. I'd always been unable to get excited about things. Maybe you just have to find your niche and then you can find happiness, however cold you might have supposed yourself to be beforehand. I was grateful to the crowd, for feeding me their energy, so I could feel something. People think life is easier for you whenever you don't have the ability to feel, but I think that remaining at an emotional baseline all the time is hard to deal with too. You don't have to deal with any big emotions, but you spend your life pretending that you do, just to fit in whenever you're forced into contact with others.

I didn't like to think of myself as a sociopath, but maybe I am. At least, I was whenever I stepped off the stage. Regular life was too disappointing compared with performing. It was dull and underwhelming. I found the things that came along to lift our spirits so mediocre, I could barely conjure up a smile for them. Whenever I had my guitar strap wrapped around me, I felt like I could feel — like humans are supposed to feel. It was a good job that Clodagh wasn't there. If she was, she'd think I was "cured" and that I'd accessed my emotions. I wasn't emotionally available; I was musically available, in whatever way people needed me to be. So long as I got my fix on stage, I felt generous in spirit, for a short time.

Halfway through the gig, I noticed a woman in the crowd. She had blonde angel hair like Clodagh's, but she had a better face. It was less pretty, but much more sensible. She didn't have that dopey, lost look that came over Clodagh all the time. But then I saw her expression change. It felt unlikely that our eyes could meet through the powerful spotlights, but somehow, they did.

I saw her crumple to the floor. I didn't know if she had fainted, collapsed or sat down by choice, but one thing was clear to me: it was my job to go to her aid. I took my guitar off and jumped from the stage, pushing through the crowd to get to her. Whenever I did, I lifted her and cradled her in my arms, carrying her to the side of the stage. I set her on the steps, and I realised that she was conscious. She gazed at me lovingly and didn't release me from her grip. The audience clapped and screamed. I didn't know why they were making such a big deal out of a basic act of kindness. I was doing the right thing, like I had for Clodagh at the window that night. I hadn't when she'd been in the same position at our gig that evening, but that was a different story.

The girl stayed on the steps, to make sure her temperature was normal, and it didn't happen again. We finished up the gig, with her staring at me the entire time. I could feel her gaze burning through me. I tried to avoid it and focus on playing. I pulled it off, but it was difficult. There was a major difference between being casually watched by hundreds of people and being stared at by a single person. I knew she was single, from the way she regarded me. My gesture had unleashed problems I couldn't have anticipated. I just wanted to be a good guy, but I was inviting problems too. You had to be careful whom you helped; some people are like leeches as soon as you give them a passing look.

We finished up the gig and I hurried to get off the stage, but people were calling for an encore. We'd given one everywhere else to date, so we couldn't leave them with less. We'd already lost a few minutes of the gig thanks to the interruption. She looked like she was in excellent health, and I wondered if her fall was engineered for my attention. But I didn't want to think like that. I had to be there for the fans, the way they were there for me. If I lost them, or fell out of favour, we were all fucked. No other word could express the danger of the position we'd find ourselves in.

At least, after that night, we could walk away – on to another location, and only true devotion would cause a fan to follow you that far. We weren't famous yet. We didn't have fans that were that devoted yet. Maybe one day we would. Maybe we'd be followed and stalked, and I'd even like it.

Chapter Twenty-Five

After the gig, the girl pounced on me. Her name was Diana, and she was a predator – I could tell as soon as she started talking. Her shrinking violet act vanished as soon as she opened her mouth. She had a deep, commanding voice with the crackle that comes from heavy smoking. I didn't have that, for some reason, and I knew I never would. I was just one of those people that gets to do what they like, and they always get away with it, escaping the consequences. I could already feel her fangs sinking into me, but I could throw her off and speed off in the minivan. She wasn't coming with us, whatever she thought. She probably put together the act, hoping one of us would be gullible enough to fall for it, and then she'd follow us like a groupie with an agenda. I knew I needed to get as far away from her as I could, as quickly as possible. Was it some sort of karmic connection? Like life's revenge for my treatment of Clodagh? I reminded myself that I didn't believe in any of that stuff.

She was hanging around, limply, like she was waiting for something to happen, but it never would. I knew I wasn't that way inclined. I never felt tempted to sleep with someone just for the sake of it. That wasn't some sort of noble decision made out of concern for another person's feelings; I just didn't see the point or feel the need for it. The others were surprisingly loyal to their girlfriends. I didn't witness a moment's disloyalty. We were an odd-looking bunch, so I didn't exactly expect the offers to come flooding in, but there's a certain allure that comes with being in a band. Women that would ordinarily refuse your gaze in the street were suddenly signing up for first place on your list. Options were aplenty. Maybe they just wanted to be able to say they'd bedded some musician before they made it to fame. I hadn't known that groupies still existed, but it turned out they did, in vast quantities.

I just wanted some space to myself. The gigging wasn't the problem; it was the overcrowded van. It was claustrophobic, but I still would have chosen to remain there forever with my pals rather than having to share a bed with another Clodagh for a single night.

The gig went glossily smoothly. We knew the setlist inside out and back to front by then. It was like the most intensive practice session. We were under pressure to play our best every single night. The speaker systems in those places wouldn't have hidden any musical sins. We had to play as close to perfect as we were capable of doing. I was up for the challenge. I just doubted the stamina of the others. All in all, they were a lazy group. They probably would have done anything to get out of having to do a regular job. They did have jobs in pubs and restaurants back in Glasgow. Everyone joked with me that I was the master at evading work. But they weren't exactly committed to their jobs either. I still felt like I was the only serious musician in the band. No one else tinkered around with songs post or pre-gig. The rest were there to have a laugh with some friends and to pass the time, with the added benefit of being unreachable in terms of fulfilling a job contract. I didn't know how long the novelty would last for. I knew that Greg was very attached to Deborah. She was his favourite person – he'd made that clear. He always said she came first, even whenever he was having to put her last for the sake of the band. I knew he'd always return to her. He wouldn't be happy with a life spent forever on the road.

The girl that had the fainting episode made a point of giving me her number. She tried to invite herself along on the rest of the tour, but I used our tour bus as an excuse. We could barely breathe on board as it was. We didn't have room for another passenger – especially one as clingy as her. Knowing her for less than an hour had already shown me so many aspects to her character that I didn't like. I was thankful that I was single. Some people might have seen me as a loner, but I saw myself as free. We made our getaway in the minibus, and I hoped she'd never attend another one of our gigs again. Sadly, you can't control who the ticket buyers are. If they pay for the ticket and they haven't done anything illegal, what can you do to stop them?

Chapter Twenty-Six

Greg woke me up early the next morning. I'm not used to being roused from my sleep. I haven't slept with an alarm in a long time. I always hated them. It's a miracle I stayed in school as long as I did. I've never liked to disrupt my body's natural sleep cycles. I don't think it's good for the human body. It wasn't how nature intended things to be. We were never meant to have desk jobs, to use cars more than our legs, to be dissolved into someone else's being rather than standing alone in our own.

Greg looked panicked whenever I looked at him, but nothing much fazed me anymore – not since the window incident. Nothing ever had, when it came to problems other people freak out about – I'm just not easily disturbed. The things that disturb me are more self-focused, like interruptions to my desired routine, running out of tobacco whenever the shop isn't open yet, breaking a guitar string when I haven't got any spare ones handy. I've never been ruffled by the problems of others – at least not until they're right in my face and I'm made responsible for them. I would do anything to avoid being implicated in something, and I've learned that people are unpredictable; you never know what they might do next, what they might blame you for next.

"I got a message from Deborah," he said.

I could tell he was tiptoeing around the subject; that he was going to work his way to the main point gradually. I just wanted to get to the root of it right away.

"What happened?"

"It was about Clodagh – I know you broke up and you don't like talking about her – but she went back to Ireland."

"To live?"

I felt relief filling me up, combined with guilt. She'd had an entire life established in Scotland, and I knew that I was the reason for her leaving. She might have come up with a thousand other reasons, but I was the one that had precipitated the whole thing. Without me, I knew she'd still be happily living in Scotland.

"Her flatmates think it's permanent. They said she was in a bad way."

I was hardly surprised; she was always in a bad way. I knew the stories about her jewellery-making and her false happiness were fabricated. She couldn't have adapted so easily to our break-up. She was too invested in us –

in what she thought we were. I'd never been the person she thought I was, but she'd seen the good in me. She'd found it through sheer strong will. I knew I should say something, but I didn't know what would suffice. There was nothing I could say that would pardon my behaviour.

"Why did she leave?"

I tried to sound casual, like I didn't have anything to do with it. I wanted everyone to think that I'd had nothing to do with it. I had no idea what Susie thought of me now. It shouldn't have mattered, but I'd always got on well with her. If we happened to bump into each other, I wanted that easy rapport to continue, even just for the sake of social comfort. I didn't want to perch awkwardly next to her on a shared sofa at a party, unable to find a word to say to her. Worse; I didn't want her to confront me about my lack of care for Clodagh. On some level, I knew she was probably on my side, at least a little bit. She'd lived with Clodagh; she knew what she was like. She'd missed a day's work and a day's pay just to take her to hospital for her amateur theatrics. Clodagh had probably left on purpose, just to create a stir. She wouldn't be happy in Ireland either. She didn't deserve to be. Even if she did have a good heart – basically – the window incident had been unforgiveable. What worse parting could a person think of? It would remain in my memory for ever – even if I made every effort to crush it each time it resurfaced. You can't unsee something like that; especially if you've been forced to become an active participant in it.

"She wasn't happy in Glasgow. I think the break-up was hard on her, but she had other issues too."

"Such as?"

"You dated her, didn't you? You'd know better than me."

"Some people are hard to figure out."

Clodagh certainly wasn't one of them. She wore every one of her feelings displayed on her sleeve, like it was an embellishment she was proud to show off. But I wanted to appear like the innocent party – the ignorant ex-boyfriend that had no idea about the suffering she had gone through. She was a lost cause – someone for whom no amount of care could make a difference. That was the story I was sticking with. Some people try to wind themselves around your neck like a noose, and you have no choice but to shake them off you, before they tighten the loop and choke you beyond redemption.

I wouldn't allow myself to feel guilty about someone that had caused something so traumatic to happen to me. If I'd been a normal, feeling person,

I probably would have forever been destroyed by it. As things stood, the memory of it bothered me. It hung over me and clung to me like Clodagh's limpet-like grip.

I was free of her, and I didn't want to hear another story about her. I didn't need updates on her life. I preferred to pretend to myself that she'd fallen from that window, that I'd called 999 but it had been too late. I wished I'd played the part of the doting, devastated boyfriend – the one that arrived to find his suicidal girlfriend motionless on the concrete below her raised window.

"Can we stop talking about Clodagh?" I asked Greg.

"Yeah, sorry – I just thought you'd want to know."

"Why would I want to know? We broke up."

"I don't know – I'd want to know if that happened to Deborah."

"You love Deborah. You're still with Deborah."

"Sorry, I guess I misread the situation. Will we get a pint before the gig to lift our spirits?"

My spirit felt so low it was getting grazed on the ground, but it wasn't because I loved Clodagh. I was just haunted by her. I wished I'd never gone along for drinks on the night we'd met. I'd opened a can of worms that could never again be resealed.

Chapter Twenty-Seven

We played in Scarborough next. It was a place I'd only ever seen on TV. It wasn't somewhere I ever thought I'd play my electric guitar. I thought of it as a holiday destination for the elderly, but it was beautiful. The tour was exposing me to things I hadn't even anticipated. It was opening me up to different versions of living I had never entertained. I'd been limited by the city of Glasgow. I had a place for it in my heart, but its grey gloom weighed on me. The more time I spent away from it, the more I didn't want to return. It was a place of musical opportunity, but I felt like we had got as far as we could there. I didn't know if I'd ever go back, even if my bandmates did. Maybe I could continue with my life on the run. On the run from what, I couldn't say. Clodagh wasn't in Glasgow anymore. I no longer ran the risk of running into her. She had given me back my city of birth and she wasn't trespassing on it anymore. I could even hang out in the West End, and she wouldn't be there. She might have haunted me in the associations I'd built up, but gladly, most of our memories together were contained in that now-vacant flat. I heard that Sarah had gone travelling abroad and Susie had moved in with her boyfriend. Maybe the new occupants would clear the air; they'd have no idea what happened there before they'd arrived.

I missed the comfort and privacy of my own flat, and the fact that I could go days without speaking to anyone there if I wanted to. We were all like ships passing in the night. I was paying my rent for then – or the Housing Executive was, anyway. I planned to go back to it at some point. I just wanted the tour to last for as long as it possibly could, until we had another one lined up. It was good to know I had a base to return to whenever I needed to. I hoped once we amassed more money, we could invest in a proper tour bus. The van was fine for the time being, but it wouldn't work permanently. I could stand it, for the sake of getting to do what I wanted to do. I'd told the job centre I would be away over the summer, so I didn't even have to check in with the lady whose name I had already forgotten to tick off my list. I thought about asking her to just do me the favour of marking me off without me having to come in in future. I could tell her it was breaking me and destroying my confidence, coming to those meetings for so long. It would do that to anyone's spirit – anyone with a normal desire to work anyway. I wasn't that, but she would never think that. She was too won over by my innocent looks and my underfed appearance. She probably wished she could take over from my mother and give me the care I really needed. I was glad my mother was much more distant than that. That kind of smothering from a family member would have driven me out of the country for good.

Speaking of care, I was starving. There was nothing to consume in the van apart from a half-eaten KitKat, and some energy drinks. I needed something more substantial than that. I asked the others if they were hungry too and we all went to a chip shop. We sat in and I got fish and chips and ate it hungrily, seated at the window table. We didn't talk to each other; we just ate. We were all famished. Maybe it was the result of expending so much energy on gigging and keeping the hunger pangs away with nothing but chocolate and sporadic sandwiches. I guess we all need to care for ourselves at some point, but the life on the road suited my personality. I didn't feel tied to anything. I felt like I'd been released from the irritating obligations I had to fulfil at home. Even without a job, annoyingly, they still existed.

With full bellies, we went back to our tour bus. We got into our cramped quarters and slept like the dead. The gig had taken everything out of us. We didn't stir, even with friends' feet in our faces. Everybody's idea of heaven is different, and I was in mine, apart from the fact Greg's foot odour was wafting into my nostrils. At least none of them snored like Clodagh did.

Chapter Twenty-Eight

Next, Leeds was on the agenda. The crowd was very subdued, but maybe they weren't excited about us yet because we were still a small band. Our name was out there, more than it had been before the summer, but our reputation didn't precede us yet. We played good gigs, but we didn't break any laws and we didn't have enough of a fanbase to create a stir. That would come with time; I was confident of that. I never saw myself becoming someone that caused societal unrest though. I was too much of a quiet, book-reading type to do that. I liked to live quietly. I just wanted to express myself through music. The music could speak for itself. We didn't need to act rashly or unlawfully to generate interest in our band. Time was all we needed – that and consistent gigging.

Greg was moping around before the gig. I didn't have time for his attitude. It wasn't the energy we needed onstage. He said he missed Deborah too much and that he wanted to go home. They had just moved in with each other, and she had a friend staying over the summer to keep her company while he was away. He'd phoned her devotedly every day, gladly out of earshot of the rest of us. Their romance disgusted me. I didn't understand it at all. Neither of them was completely conventional in the boring sense, so why did they follow society's romantic templates so strictly? Love was a waste of time, as far as I was concerned. It didn't give you a reason for living like music did. I didn't want him to be distracted from the band, or from our main aim, and it felt like his flowery romance was getting in the way of that. I decided to have a word with him, about his commitment to the band.

Jake was still always hanging around in the background, talking incessantly and bossing us about. He was getting on my nerves too, because he couldn't play a note, but he thought he was qualified to lead the band. He was good at talking, which I guess was a good thing when it came to selling tickets, but his arrogance got to me. I was glad he was sitting in the passenger seat most of the time, so I could ignore him from the back of the van.

Leeds welcomed us, but only with applause. I couldn't wait for the day when a crowd screamed upon our arrival. It would make everything I'd sacrificed for it worthwhile – even putting up with people like Jake and Greg. They had human weaknesses. Their flaws were noticeable, but as long as we kept moving forwards as a band, I could mostly tolerate them.

I played my guitar with all the love I could direct into it and the tone was rich and rewarding. I sang my heart out, or I would have, had I had one. I put all my energy into what I was creating on stage, so I was physically spent at the end. All I had left in me was sleep, which was all we could fit into our lives in the van anyway. The guys seemed satisfied with the gig whenever it ended, but it pissed me off. They never strove to be the best. They were happy to remain at the level they were at, never learning anything new or developing themselves. The crowd gave us hearty applause, but there was no cheering, no whistles, no chants of "one more song."

I still felt like I could only go so far in that band. I probably haven't even mentioned the name of it until now. It's unremarkable, probably because the others picked it. As I said, we're called "The Turnpikes." It could have been chosen at random out of a hat, for all the time they put into choosing it. Greg thought his idea had been a stroke of genius. I would have renamed it in a heartbeat, but no one else seemed to dislike it. If only I could have been a one-man band. I had the skill, but I was annoyed with myself for lacking the confidence to get up there alone. I couldn't have talked to the microphone the way Jake did. He seduced the crowd with his Scottish rambling. They were won over by whatever he said, however nonsensical. I wasn't one to waste words; I never have been.

When we finished the gig, we got the same level of applause we got upon starting. It was disappointing that we didn't impress them more, or they might have just been a subdued crowd. It's hard to say what the cause was. Sometimes the energy just isn't as elevated. Maybe they hadn't had enough to drink or maybe we hadn't played as perfectly as I'd hoped.

Greg's girlfriend had never liked our music and she wasn't quiet about it. She came to the gigs for Greg, but we all knew she wouldn't have gone to a single one otherwise. I wanted to know what she found lacking in my songwriting. I knew I couldn't expect someone that liked radio hits to appreciate the complexity of our music, but it worried me. It made me think that others mightn't like it either. Even though our tour was going well, it didn't feel like we were an overnight success. Somewhere deep inside, I had believed that whenever we played our first big gig, word of mouth would have led to us being catapulted into fame. *The Turnpikes* were still the kind of band that had to tell everyone their name. We couldn't just walk into a room and be recognised. The introverted part of me wondered how I would adapt to true fame. I wanted appreciation for our music and a real fanbase, but I also valued my anonymity. I liked being able to go to the Tesco Express on the corner without having to exchange words with anyone I passed. I could be as antisocial as I wished. That wasn't something to take for granted. I supposed even if we did become famous, I'd be the less noticeable guitarist that lurked in the shadows – not the charismatic lead singer. We could keep to ourselves if we wanted to, staying inside the van and moving from place to place, discreetly getting supplies from shops and sending Kyle to do it on our behalf. He thought he was the driving force behind the band because he was a chatterbox and he liked to share his ideas for improvement – none of which sounded like they'd improve anything. But he wouldn't be remembered for contributing to the music; he was just a behind-the-scenes guy. I felt the same sometimes – like my efforts weren't truly praised. They just got lost in the band.

I was growing resentful, but I had no idea what was still to come. I hated when people didn't "try." I had been trying my hardest since day one, within the context of the band. I didn't deserve to be forgotten in the crowd. Part of me wanted to break free of my shyness and take charge of everything publicly.

After Leeds, we were meant to travel down to Sheffield, but that was whenever ructions appeared within the band. Greg had been avoiding me for a couple of days – as much as he could within the confines of the van. We'd stopped off to eat at a couple of picnic spots and he'd gone for long, meandering walks with no sign of returning for hours. We didn't have that amount of time to waste, so whenever he got back, I confronted him.

"Why are you going off by yourself all the time?"

"I need time to think."

"To think … about what?"

"You don't know what I'm dealing with inside my head."

"I don't but I don't think you're thinking of the band. You're just abandoning your bandmates and keeping us waiting around for you to return from your long walks. I need to know if you're in or out."

"Who appointed you band manager?" he asked, callously.

"I write all our stuff, don't I?" I said.

I'd never thrown that in his face before, but it suddenly felt like it was time to. He needed a reminder of my importance in the band. I wasn't just a faceless guitar player. I was brimming with ideas, constantly. He needed to wake up to what was happening. He wasn't just not being a bandmate; he wasn't being a friend. Being on the road was tough on everyone, in its own way, but he needed to air his problems – not remove himself from the band.

The others were talking about getting on the road again. We needed to if we wanted to make good time, but I knew I needed to finish talking to Greg. I was his best friend, and I knew he'd confide in me much more readily than any of the others. He knew I'd never repeat what he said either. I might have been many things, but I wasn't a gossip, and I knew how to keep a secret, forever.

I told the others I needed to talk to Greg in private and we went on a walk of our own. Whenever we were in the peace of nature, away from all the shouting and messing around of the others, I could hear his anxiety. He was noticeably shaky, and he was stumbling over his words.

"I can't do it," he said.

"Can't do what?"

"Play."

"You've been doing it every day. It's just the same routine all over again – in a different place. I think you're doing great."

I swallowed as I said it because I knew it was, at least partially, a lie.

"It's not just that – it's not just playing – it's the band."

"What about it?"

"I can't do it anymore."

"Why?"

"Touring is killing me. I can't stand being away from Deborah for this long."

"You'll see her at the end of the summer – it isn't for ever."

"That's such a long time to me. When you love someone, you want to see them every day."

I didn't understand that feeling. How could anyone feel the need to have someone around on a daily basis? How could you cease to function in someone's absence? It just sounded so sentimental and unrealistic to me. I didn't envy him. He was in a state, whether it was caused by her or not. I doubted it really could be. He must have got stage fright or started to overthink the next gig. Maybe he'd realised we were getting progressively further from home, and it had hit him. Being in a van for weeks with anyone was enough to drive a person to distraction. It didn't matter how well you knew each other, or how much you got along.

"You're probably tired of being in such a small space with everyone."

"It isn't that."

"How do you know?"

"Because my heart aches. I miss her, man."

It was sickening, really, seeing his dependency on a woman I didn't consider to be particularly special. She couldn't even appreciate good music. She didn't deserve his pining.

"What do you want to do?" I asked. "Could you video call her?"

"No, man, I've been thinking – when I get back, I want to stay for good."

"Don't you like your freedom?" I asked. I didn't understand his homesickness, nor did I know what to say to alleviate it.

"It'll be ok," I said, "You can play Sheffield and then see how you feel."

We still had many gigs left. We hadn't made it out of Northern England yet and he was already desperate to get out. I knew that he wouldn't stay much longer. If he did, it would only because I'd persuaded him to. I didn't think I'd be much of a friend if I did that. He was obviously unhappy. His eyes looked hollowed out and he looked smaller than his usual six-foot three broad frame. It was like the weight was dropping off him at the rate that his happiness was.

We walked back to the van and climbed in, our bodies bent into uncomfortable configurations, but that was nothing new. We'd get to stretch out and get our exercise on stage that night. I patted Greg on the back, even though I've never been one for making physical contact with friends. Maybe the gesture would reassure him that I was there for him – that I saw his sadness, even if I didn't understand it.

That night we hit the stage. The rest of us were in a great mood, but Greg was dragging the mood south. He was teary and he'd been beyond reluctant to step on stage. He didn't even bring his bass. I'd had to remind him to run back to get it. He was a mess. He'd been drinking straight from a bottle of Jack Daniels since 4pm. Granted, that wasn't uncommon for a band member, but he'd had more than he could handle. I could tell because he seemed so top heavy, and I was waiting for him to topple over on top of one of us. The others were all stone-cold sober which made his intoxication more apparent. I wanted to warn him not to mess up the gig, but I knew that would probably tip him over the edge and he'd refuse to go on at all. You can play without a bass player, but the depth of the music is lost, and that was important to me. The compositions I'd written required every member to carry them off. They were written for a band of four - not for a trio. I wished I could snap him out of it, but we had to work with what we had.

I played an extended intro to get him time to settle himself onstage. It felt like my moment of glory had come. I was so distracted by not wanting the performance to fall apart that I didn't mind taking centre stage and letting everyone follow my lead. The others joined in, and we jammed in a way that smoothly led into the song. Stevie was solid, and my guitar sounded great. Greg tuned his bass, and I turned my amp up so I could drown out his bum notes.

He was too wobbly to be there. I waved someone over and asked for a chair. It ruined the look of the band, but it was better than having him fall off the stage.

The performance was ridiculously bad. Not only was Greg missing every note; he was playing out of time, so he was ruining everyone else's playing too. He had become a liability to us. Maybe he was looking for a passage out of the band, and he thought if he messed up our gigs, he'd be forced to quit. Apart from his poor playing, he was a huge distraction. He was swaying in his seat, and I was waiting for something to happen. He was such a big guy that if he fell, he'd probably do serious damage to himself.

Halfway through the gig, my concerns materialised. Greg collapsed to the floor, banging his bass on the stage as he fell. Reverb pierced everyone's ears and the crowd made a collective sound of complaint. I whipped my guitar off and ran to his aid. He hadn't just fallen over; he was unconscious. He'd obviously had far too much to drink. I yelled at someone to call an ambulance, and while they did, I tried to get him to respond. I shook him but there was no sign of life. He had a pulse, but I was worried he'd given himself alcohol poisoning. I turned him over onto his front and I shouted at him to wake up. He just needed a shock. I grabbed my bottle of water and flung the contents in his face. Still, nothing. I forced his mouth open and made sure his tongue wasn't obstructing his airways. I put my fingers into his mouth and forced them down his throat. I hated doing it; apart from the fact it felt like I was doing damage to my friend. Just because I didn't feel immense concern for others didn't mean I wanted to see them suffer. It was bringing up lots of prickly feelings inside me that I didn't want to deal with. But I knew the priority was to get him conscious again. I kept jabbing my fingers into his throat. His mouth felt dry, like every ounce of moisture had left it. He finally started to gag and then he threw up on the floor. I kept going, willing him to vomit more. I knew he needed it out of his system. One bout of sickness would hopefully be enough to get rid of it. He was violently sick everywhere. The crowd was silent, and they were looking on, like passersby at the scene of a car crash. They couldn't take their eyes off the pitiful scene. I felt relief flooding me. It was the same as the relief that had come to me when I'd pulled Clodagh back in the window and we'd collapsed onto the bedroom floor. Life was still inside him and the crisis was averted. The paramedics showed up and got him onto a bed with wheels. They took him into the back of the ambulance, while I hovered, waiting to ask them a thousand questions. What was wrong? Would he be ok? Where were they taking him? What did I need to do? Could I go with him? Was he dehydrated?

They flew through the answers to every one of my questions, but I couldn't process a single answer. My mind was as noisy as a bus station at rush hour. I couldn't hear a thing. I was just terrified: terrified that Greg would die, terrified that he'd never fully recover, terrified that it meant the breakup of our band and the end of the tour. The last worry didn't overwhelm the others; they were of equal importance.

The paramedics gave me permission to come with him, so I jumped into the ambulance. I asked the others to get my guitar and amp. I knew they wouldn't just leave it behind, but I wanted them to give it the care I would have. I sat beside Greg, and I held his hand. I never thought we'd be in that position, but I didn't think I'd ever see him on the verge of death either. He was obviously afraid. I could read the fear in his eyes, even through his tough Glaswegian exterior. He looked like a small child trapped in an oversized man's body. I reassured him everything would be ok, even though I had no proof it would be. The paramedics were being evasive. They didn't like to make definitive statements in case they came back to haunt them in a lawsuit later. We got to hospital, and they wheeled him inside. I was told to wait outside, so I hung around for a long time. I knew I'd be waiting hours, but it didn't matter. The gig was already unsalvageable, so I had nowhere else to be. He was my best friend. He would have done the same for me. I didn't know why he'd done it to himself. Maybe he was as miserable on tour as he'd told me he was. He wasn't a reliable bandmate; that much was certain.

After hours of waiting, I was informed that his hydration levels had stabilised. He still wasn't well, and he'd have to be kept in until the next day, but he was out of the danger zone. I was allowed to go and see him, so I walked to his ward.

He was lying in bed in a hospital gown. He looked a special kind of exhausted. I sat on the seat at the end of the bed.

"They tell me you saved me, man," he said. "I'm sorry I put you in that position – I was just so unhappy. I didn't mean to drink so much."

He was stumbling over his words, and he looked like he could burst into tears at any moment. I'd never seen him cry before. I'd seen him sad, but he'd never shed a tear, as far as I knew. He was obviously unstable and shaken by the entire experience. He needed to go home. I wished my other bandmates were there so we could talk about it. Would we find a replacement for him? Could we send him home without the whole band having to accompany him? Maybe he could go by plane once he was feeling a bit better. We'd made enough money to pay for his flight, even if it left us with less money afterwards. We didn't require much for our survival. The main difficulty would be finding his replacement whilst we were on the road. How would we get anyone to audition? Should we just do an open call for a bassist at one of our gigs? Maybe that was the best way to find someone. We already knew they had decent taste in music if they were there to hear us, so that was a good start.

I was running ahead of myself. For then, I was stuck at Greg's bedside, filling in for Deborah. She didn't even know what had happened yet. Greg asked me to contact her for him. I didn't even have her phone number. I'd never had a reason to contact her. But Greg told me to use his phone. I knew it would just worry her and make her feel powerless because she wasn't nearby and couldn't do anything. The last thing I wanted was for her to come and join us and squeeze into the already overcrowded tour bus. He didn't need a mascot; he needed to go home. We couldn't depend on him anymore. He was too much of a flight risk.

I waited for him to be discharged, sleeping on and off in the bedside chair. The nurses didn't make me leave. I was his nominated person, so I was allowed to be there day and night. Greg slept fitfully. He appeared to have the same nightmare, over and over. I heard fragments of it – the same story told and retold. He was poisoned with alcohol, but the ending had been different. It had been final. He was talking in his sleep and fighting himself in his dream.

Whenever his fluid levels were fine and he was back to his normal self, he was allowed to be discharged. I called the others and they said they'd pick us up at the door. They'd waited up all night, they said, talking about all the possible outcomes and blaming themselves for their part in it. We stayed in the metal waiting chairs, with Greg questioning the meaning of life out loud. It wasn't exactly enjoyable, and I was desperate to get out of there and put the entire thing behind us. I was feeling differently about our friendship. I'd used up all the sympathy I could muster the previous night, and now, I was just getting irritated by him. I didn't know why he couldn't just pull it together for the sake of the band. It was selfish of him - the man that had once called me the most selfish man he'd ever met. Maybe he'd really been thinking of himself whenever he said that. He could hardly say it again after that long night when I'd sacrificed lifelong dreams of mine just for him.

Back on the bus, everything wasn't what I'd expected it to be. I thought the others would have already lined up replacement bassists in my absence, but they hadn't lifted a finger. Kyle kept talking about the fact that we needed to get Greg home. He said he needed to phone all the venues and tell them we had to postpone because of a near tragedy in the band. We weren't a big name or a headliner, so no one would really notice, he said. All the talk he'd done about how big we were going to be and how the band was basically a brotherhood had gone out the window. Maybe his idea of brotherhood was different to mine. I thought it meant that we stuck together and kept playing no matter what. He thought it meant we stuck together, even if it meant we didn't play. That was my sole reason for being there: to play music. I wasn't there for the people, or for the adventure, or for any other motivation. The music came first for me, like it always had. Now I knew that the fatally flawed band I'd been in had never been serious. My misgivings had been right. They were all prepared to pack it in over one member checking out.

"What do you want to do after we drop Greg home? It's not like any of the places will have us back after cancelling our first gig."

"Isn't Greg's health more important? There will always be another gig."

I doubted the truth of that. I thought they were all giving up. Maybe it had been too much work for them, or it had taken more than they'd anticipated, and they'd arranged the whole thing – an elaborate plan to get us back to Glasgow. Most of the guys were in dead-end jobs, working in run down bars that didn't look like their doors would remain open for many more years, but apparently, that was preferable to what we were doing. This is why I've always believed that putting people first is a mistake. If you make people the primary focus of your existence, you will always be let down. They're too changeable and unpredictable, and you can't count on them. But you can count on a guitar. Even if the specific guitar you own breaks, you still have all that knowledge and talent stored up inside you, ready to be released on another instrument. People abandon you. Musical knowledge does not.

Greg seemed much more content, now that the band were discussing returning home. I was the only one that seemed resistant to their plan. Their defeatist attitude was annoying me. I wished I could kick them all off the bus, recruit a new band, and let them make their own way home. My charitable, friendly act the previous night had achieved nothing. We were finished.

Chapter Twenty-Nine

We were on the road, heading North rather than South and I hadn't spoken a word to anyone in hours. I didn't know what to say, so I just slept on and off. Everything in my being was fighting against our journey back to Scotland, but I was outnumbered and everyone else seemed relieved to be going home. They all had girlfriends they were probably dying to see. Kyle believed his act of driving home was heroic. He was prioritising his friend's health and wellbeing over money and the chance to make it big. I was loathing Greg more with each mile we travelled. It was his fault that we weren't performing that night, and I'd got the bug – the need to perform on a daily basis. I thought of my life in Glasgow and how depressing it would be in comparison to that. We'd probably disband after we got there, citing reasons of ill health. Then, and maybe only then, would it become possible to get gigging with a different band. I knew *The Turnpikes* wouldn't continue without Greg, and there was no point in him being there if we ended up stuck in the studio and we could only play within a three mile radius of his flat. I wondered how our friendship could possibly survive a betrayal as big as this one. He'd ruined my life's dream in one night. The drive was interminable. It felt different without stopping to play along the way. We stopped for bathroom breaks and to eat, but that was it. Kyle was powering down the motorway, like we were still living in a state of emergency.

The scenes out the window weren't as inspiring in reverse; we'd seen them before, and then, I'd been in a much better frame of mind. It took us what felt like forever to get home. Whenever I did, I opened the door to find an empty flat. My flatmates had taken a couple of weeks off work to go and see their families, and I was alone. Normally, that would have been a beautiful feeling, but I gladly would have sacrificed my personal space to keep playing. The flat felt strangely quiet. I blasted some Springsteen and made myself an espresso: the usual routine. I didn't know what to do with myself. I would have played my guitar, but it was only a reminder of the crushing disappointment I was feeling – not that I needed a reminder; it was all I could think about. People that say trials come before success are probably only able to appreciate that after the event. I was at my lowest point – lower than after the loss of any person. I could have kept playing, but what was the point whenever no one was there to hear it? I pulled the curtains in my room and got into bed. I felt truly sorry for myself, and I felt no inclination to bother with my bandmates again. You can always make new friends, but you can't as easily find another viable band. A band is a special concoction, and it's close to impossible to get it right.

Chapter Thirty

Greg was phoning me, repeatedly. I hadn't answered once. Whatever had once made him my best friend had dissolved between us. There was no reason to talk, so I rolled over in bed, facing the rented, blank wall. I'd never felt the need to decorate it. It was just functional, and I probably wouldn't be there forever, even though it felt like I would in that moment. Finally, when I could rest no more, I got up. I walked to the corner shop to get some tobacco. I had hardly any money left for all my efforts. It had been used up on Greg. I was resentful. I couldn't help the feeling; it overcame me. I knew they'd all fall back into their old routine, like the tour had never happened, like we hadn't been a no-show at about ten gigs. Some people join bands to make it as musicians, while others do it to bide time. I knew the truth about my bandmates and there was no turning back.

I needed a change of scenery. I wanted to go to the West End and treat myself to a coffee and a new book. It was good to know I could go there now without running the risk of encountering Clodagh. If she'd still been living there, I probably never would have set foot in the place again. I got off the subway, coming out of the mouth of the station and up into daylight, like I was emerging from a lengthy entrapment. I walked in the direction of Clodagh's old street. I was dying for a coffee from the French café, and maybe a baguette. I could taste it before I'd come within a close enough proximity to smell it. I rounded the corner, and I was surprised to find that the place was vacant. The lettering on the sign had been removed and a "to let" sign had been plastered over it. He must have left, but I didn't know when, and I never would because my connections to that street were gone. I walked to the next café – the one that sat directly below the old flat, and I ordered myself a double espresso. It was more expensive than the French café, but it was more popular too. I didn't think it was anywhere near as good. I got my coffee to go and continued walking the streets, heading in the direction of a great second-hand book shop I knew. The weather was surprisingly good for Glasgow. The sun shone on the city with an uncharacteristic strength. Kelvingrove park was overrun with people – mostly students being loud and obnoxious. I was glad I never belonged to that social group. I was running ideas through my head – ideas of survival. I would have to start searching for a new band, or I'd drive myself to distraction. I was just unclear as to how I would set one up; maybe I'd have to join an already existent one. I just hoped they'd be open-minded enough to accept my songs.

I walked up Gibson Street and took a right at the corner. I entered the lane with the tea house in it: the one that Clodagh loved. I could feel her energy in that little lane. It was so strange. I've never really had any experiences like that before, but it hit me like a speeding bus. She might have been in another country, but her spirit was still very much there. I tried to ignore it so I could go to the bookshop, but it was impossible to ignore it, so I walked to *Fopp* instead. I'd always found plenty of Murakami there anyway, for just a couple of pounds. It didn't matter if I couldn't return to that lane. How much time had I spent there anyway? I had never set foot in the place with Clodagh. We'd never gone out for tea or coffee, or dined out, or gone shopping together. We'd barely gone anywhere. Her room had been the homebase for our relationship. I was glad we hadn't ventured much further. It was a big city, but at least I didn't have to run into people I barely knew and have them question where Clodagh went. I shook her off me, like a spider web I'd inadvertently walked through. I paced around the West End, heading to my alternative choice of bookshop and stocking up on any books by Murakami they had in stock. I never found another author that appealed to me as much. His books entertained me without demanding too much from me. Clodagh told me she liked him too, but she'd only ever had one copy of his book on her bookshelf: *Kafka by the Shore*. It was my favourite one, but I doubted she'd even read it, so thankfully, I didn't associate it with her.

I got what I needed and got the subway home. The weather meant the parks were so full that you couldn't have found a bench or even a patch of grass to peacefully sit on. I preferred whenever they were dead, even if they might have been called "creepy" at that point. I'd never enjoyed being around large numbers of people, unless they're standing beneath me when I'm on a stage. I guess that was one of the things that had drawn Clodagh to me; she wasn't hugely outgoing either. I didn't know why I was even entertaining any thoughts of her, however trivial. I thought I'd detached from her for good, and hearing that she had left Glasgow had finalised it – or it was meant to. I couldn't control the triggers that led to her entering my mind. Sometimes I wondered if she'd wanted it to be like that. All the emails she'd sent me after we broke up led me to believe that she wanted to keep her claws hooked into me. It was over, however hard she'd wanted to cling on. I'd ended it and there was nothing she could have done to change it.

It felt like life in Glasgow was over. I was just killing time, waiting for the next opportunity to come along. I checked in at the benefits office with Fiona. She was noticeably pleased to see me, and she signed me off and sent me on my merry way. I still had a small income, but I was dying to get back into gigging. Once you find your life's purpose, it's hard to turn your back on it, even temporarily.

Greg continued to contact me, but I didn't pick up and I didn't respond to his messages. He seemed genuinely confused as to why I wasn't talking to him. He could be idiotic in that way. He probably thought I'd always have his back because I was the one that had it that night, but he hadn't upheld his part of the deal. In a way, it was a relief to cut off from that group of individuals. I'd never enjoyed their girlfriends as company and Deborah was a pain. I was ready for new doors to open to me, and to get a chance to see what was behind them, I had to close the old doors first.

For two days, I felt sorry for myself and lay around reading my books and disappearing into fictional worlds. I didn't give much thought to reality, other than interruptions for bathroom breaks, espresso and food. I could live like a bachelor since my flatmates were still on holiday, and I realised how beautiful that was. I didn't feel lonely or bored; I felt how I was meant to feel in my most natural state: alone.

People always talk about loneliness like it's a bad thing. They express their pity for strangers they see dining alone or attending a film screening alone. But why do they never stop to think, what if the person is happier like that? Maybe they don't like inane conversation to interfere with their enjoyment of said activities. There's no better feeling than walking down a sunny street, the sun hanging over the back of your head and only one long shadow stretching out in front of you. It's easier to define who you are then. In a group, you all become jumbled, and no one knows what they like anymore, or who they are.

I know from reading and listening to people talking that most people reminisce whenever something comes to an end, but I've never done that. I might get sporadic thoughts and pieces of memories. But I never sit and romanticise what once was. Maybe I just find it easy to cut off from people. They're easily replaceable; whereas my own contentment is something for which no substitution exists.

There was a heatwave that week. It was abnormally hot and close in the city. The air felt like it was a solid mass. There was no breeze and no relief. I don't own any summer clothes, so it was best to remain inside, shaded from it all. It didn't matter how unusual and how spectacular the sunshine was; I was made to be a hermit.

Chapter Thirty-One

I needed to get out of Glasgow, and fast. But there was nowhere obvious to go to and no money to fund it. I didn't want to demean myself by going to auditions. It felt like I shouldn't have to as the writer of so many songs, but sometimes you have no other choice, and I wanted to be in a successful band more than anything. I had no attachment to my home, or to my city, or to my family. I was the perfect person for life on the road. Even after doing it for a very short time, I knew it was the right lifestyle for me. I hated that I was wasting time in a situation I didn't want to be in. Nothing else had ever motivated me to get off the dole for good. As I told you, I'd had a job a year or two earlier working on video games. It had been a cool job, but even that hadn't motivated me to keep working. I quit eventually because the early starts weren't for me. No one else seemed to mind them, but I couldn't keep it up. It's hard being an unsettled person expected to lead a settled existence.

When I looked at ads online for guitarists wanted, it was overwhelming seeing the sheer volume of spaces in bands. There was no way to know whether they were talented or terrible unless I went down there. Each band sold themselves well, but that didn't mean there was anything worth selling. I arranged to meet one later that night at the studio they rehearsed at. They said they'd meet me outside. I didn't see their photos, but I didn't think it would be easy to miss them. They already had a name and a style. That put me off. I didn't want to come in like someone on the backfoot. I wanted to be the leader in the band – the pioneer. I knew I'd have to work my way there, but I'd quickly prove myself with my songs and my playing. I probably had more experience than all of them put together.

It felt good to put my guitar back in its case, to feel the textured handle in my grip, to take it onto the subway, like a date I was proud to show off. I descended into the subway and made it two minutes before the train was due. It burst through the tunnel in orange, the wheels grating on the tracks. It smelled like fried food and sweat, but I didn't care. I was on an important passage. Even if it wasn't the right band for me, it was a step in the right direction. I was doing something; I was making my own way in the world. They say friendships and work don't mix, and when it came to the band, I thought that was right. You might make friends with your bandmates after forming the band, but starting off as friends meant that that part always came first. The music was the thing that needed to come first.

I got off the subway and made my way up the escalator, protectively holding my guitar. It was a Les Paul and I'd paid for it with my own wages. It was precious to me. I would have defended it to the death. I suppose that was the kind of loyalty people like Clodagh were looking for in a romantic partner, but I'd never been capable of providing that for a person.

I approached the band. I could see an obvious theme to their look. They were all wearing rocker type stuff. I didn't like to be as obvious as that. They looked young and inexperienced, but you never really know until you hear a band playing together. It either clicks or it doesn't. I'd find out in the studio.

We walked into an old building that looked like it was in ruins from the outside, but inside, there was a decent studio. They paid us in and didn't ask me for a penny. I thought that was a nice touch. We dragged our instruments upstairs and offloaded them in the cramped room. The equipment was good, but the place was tiny. I didn't know how to audition. I'd never done it before it and it somehow felt like I was demeaning myself. But I had no other option.

I got my guitar plugged into the amp and got everything exactly as I liked it. I had an effects pedal, but I left it for later. You need to show you can play the basics without the frills first. I played one of my own songs and I sang, even though it pained me to do it. I've never enjoyed singing solo. If only I did, I wouldn't have had to put myself through auditions in the first place.

I finished the song and waited for their response. They didn't say much.

"Do you think you could play a recognisable cover... like, something we all know, just to see how it sounds?" asked the lead singer.

I didn't like him; I decided then and there. Why did he need to hear something he knew inside out to know whether it was any good? I picked a cover, and I played it, but I didn't feel good about it. It was a cover I liked, but it annoyed me that I had to do it, like a performing seal, ball balanced on nose and all. I'd already emotionally checked out of the experience.

They gave me a lifeless round of applause and then they gave me the usual round of compliments. I had to hear them too, but I didn't care to. I knew I should out of politeness, so I waited and let them play for me. It was underwhelming. They were in tune and in time, but there wasn't anything special about it. They were another band that would probably fall into obscurity, break up without anyone noticing and go on to become bankers and social workers and servers in coffee chains. That wasn't the future I wanted, so I wished them all well and walked out. They seemed very disappointed. I didn't know how many auditions they'd held, but I was sure there were few that they considered to be acceptable. Like every other band in the history of bands, they probably believed that they were destined to make it.

I knew I'd be going to a string of auditions and that the whole process would be incredibly frustrating, but what other choice did I have? That's what happens whenever you start a band with your friends. How many friendships survive the demise of a band anyway? I'd wasted so much time on something that amounted to nothing.

Chapter Thirty-Two

After repeating the process what felt like a hundred times, I was starting to think I'd never find the right band. I knew I needed to think positively, but it was hard to when faced with such a combined lack of talent. There was a multitude of untalented musicians out there. In a way, it assured me of my own talent because there was so little competition out there. I just needed to find the right vehicle for it.

For months on end, there was no sign of hope on the horizon. I was getting as depressed as I was capable of feeling. I wanted my efforts to pay off. I could have given up and just surrendered, living comfortably on the dole and going to my meetings with Fiona. But I wanted to make it big. I wanted to go on tour and make it as far as London, at the very least. The incomplete tour had given me a hunger for more.

One day, I was walking in the city centre, looking for some new shoes when I passed Greg. He looked at me and I looked at him. I kept walking. He slowed down, so then I knew I'd have to stop. It just felt like there was nothing to say.

"Hey, man," he said, "How are you?"

"Ok, how about you? Feeling better?"

"Yeah," he said, probably thinking "no thanks to you."

Awkwardness hung in the air.

"What are you up to today?" he asked.

Plain old small talk was all we had left; better than talking about feelings, but worse than talking about anything else.

"Just looking for some new shoes. You?"

"I have work in an hour or so. It was good to see you, man."

"You too," I said.

My insincerity was beyond obvious. I hoped we'd never run into each other again. I might have gone from spending a lot of time with him to no time at all, but that didn't upset me. What he had done upset me. There was no point addressing it. People only address things with the aim of improving a relationship or sharing their spite, but I didn't feel the need to do either, so I just kept walking without looking back. You can't look back in life, or you just hold yourself back. If you want to make it in music, you have to have a core of steel. I knew I did, and I couldn't surround myself with anyone that had too much human weakness running through them.

The Hero that Walks Away

Chapter Thirty-Three

I was passed from pillar to post in my search for a band. There were so many auditions I showed up to and no one was there. It might have spared me an earache, but it was a headache going through the journey for nothing. Finding a good band was proving more challenging than I ever would have thought. I thought about busking in town sometimes, to earn some extra cash, but I knew I wouldn't have the bravery to sing alone, and I didn't want to reduce myself to a street performer. Once you do that, it feels like you get typecast in that role. You'll be sweeping the city streets with the hems of your trousers until pneumonia takes you from the world.

I struggled to sleep, and I spent my time playing my guitar day and night. I'd written so many new songs. I've always had quick recall, so it was easy for me to remember them. They were like wasted gems, lying in an unopened jewellery box. I was dying to show them to the world. I just needed the right combination of people, and the world would see my art.

Finally, it felt like things were turning around. I went to an audition with a group of guys that knew what they were doing. I walked in, played one of my songs and they praised it.

"How the hell are you not already in a band?" asked the drummer.

They were all so friendly and encouraging. They didn't look like clones of each other either and they could play their instruments. I felt like I'd hit the jackpot. I didn't even mind contributing my fiver to the pot for the use of the studio. It was better than going in free for a band that didn't have an ounce of promise between them.

I liked the name of the band too. It was more thought-out; more "me." They called themselves *The Blackened Hearts*. It might have sounded a little sentimental if you overthought it, but I liked the gothic vibes of it. I was glad to feel like I belonged somewhere, musically. Most people want to belong in life, but that had never mattered to me. I'd never cared about making my own way, but I needed the backing of a decent band to carry me into touring again.

They already had some gigs lined up. The other guitarist was a proactive kind of guy. He was pushy enough that he managed to sort of gigs for us, but pleasant enough that people wouldn't hold it against him. The singer was a quiet, smiley sort of guy with a big voice. He was impressed with my vocals and the harmonies I sang. He said our voices complimented each other's. I knew he was getting as excited as I was about our potential. We might have been starting from scratch, but it felt like we were starting with a springboard behind us. We had the chemistry a band needs to succeed. That's the kind of thing that you can't acquire through practice; you can only improve upon it. That was the level I should have been playing at from the start; I should never have been playing around with the bottom feeders of the band world.

Chapter Thirty-Four

There was a girl, and she reminded me of Clodagh. She had her hair, her frame and her movements. It was uncanny. She happened to be casually dating a member of my new band: Dan. He didn't seem overly interested in her. I felt drawn to her, despite my better judgement, but I knew I needed to keep a safe distance. She was eyeing me, like she was sizing me up for something – probably just putting me in line as another option if things didn't go swimmingly with Dan. I needed to get out of her presence then and there, but how could I? I couldn't dictate whom we had in our company. I tried to ignore her, but it felt like she could read my thoughts. Her eyes bore through me, and I felt exposed, like she knew about Clodagh, but she couldn't have.

I hated the fact that Clodagh's name still came so quickly to my lips. It was like I'd never fallen out of the daily habit of saying it. She was an ever-presence even whenever I strove to drive her from my mind. I knew I needed to be as busy as I could possibly be with the band, to keep my mind occupied. The more time we spent playing, the less time there was to hang out with Clodagh's ghost.

The songs were all coming together: a mixture of the ones I'd written and the preexisting ones the rest of the band had composed. They went together seamlessly; it was amazing just how well they matched up. We were gig-ready, and we had a few lined up. Clodagh's clone, or rather - Amy - would be at every single one. I knew that before we even had them booked. She was the clingy kind of hanger-on that thought she was going somewhere serious with Dan, but someone needed to break it to her that he wasn't that kind of guy. He didn't want to settle down or to be in a serious situation. He wanted to be on the road for life. He was my perfect match; not hers. I couldn't wait until she vanished into obscurity. It was inevitable that she would; it was just a matter of time.

It had been a year since I'd broken up with Clodagh. I hadn't wanted it to be a defining moment in my life. I'd expected it to be forgettable, but her behaviour ensured it wasn't. I thought I'd done well to recover from it, to pick myself up and to keep moving forwards with my band goals. Many people couldn't have got over something as "traumatic" as that. I'd always taken that word with a pinch of salt. I think it's overused nowadays, and it's lost a lot of its original meaning. But that moment truly was traumatic. It was etched into my mind, and it kept coming up every time peace reigned in my head. Even from a different country and with no contact, I wasn't allowed to rest. You can quit a relationship, but you can't quit the memory of it.

Our first gig was scheduled for later that week. We worked flat out to get ready for it. We were in the studio day and night. We were there so much that the owner didn't even charge us the normal rate. We were his best clients, he said.

Whenever we showed up at the gig venue, it was disappointing. It was a bar I was unfamiliar with, situated in a back street. On a Tuesday night, I thought, we'd probably have about three people watching us. It was obvious the band had never properly gigged. They were excited about it, and they kept talking about it like it was a once in a lifetime experience. I hoped they were right. I wanted it to be over and done with so we could move on to something better.

We squeezed onto a tiny stage and set up. There was a drumkit there, but Euan was ranting that he should have brought his own. It wasn't my problem, so I let him get on with it. My amp and mic were working just fine; that was all that mattered. We ran through our setlist. After the set-up time, we only had ten minutes of playing time left. It was all so unremarkable, and it lay beneath us, like a rug too dirtied to even tread on. I tried my best to hide my disapproval, but it was hard to do that whenever it was shouting inside me. Whenever we started playing, the few filled tables emptied, and they approached the stage. One guy was head-banging, which I took to be a good sign. I played my best, even though the place didn't deserve it and the people weren't invested enough in us to care beyond that night. Even whenever you're completely alone, I think it's still a good idea to play your very best. You don't want to look back with regret on anything, and you never know how something small might lead to something big. The older guys seemed to appreciate our music. The younger ones must have been looking for radio hits because they seemed uninterested and continued to shout amongst themselves. Their lack of respect irritated me, but I know you have to start at the bottom and work your way up, and we would quickly do the latter.

We were proud of ourselves, and the older members of the crowd expressed their approval, citing eighties bands we were happy to be compared to. I was going to achieve my goal, and I wanted a deadline to be placed on it. I'd laid the groundwork, and I was ready for the big pay-off.

In the weeks that followed, we gigged most nights. We didn't stop to take a breath. We all got to sleep late in the mornings, and we had the energy of twenty-somethings, so it didn't do us any harm. I was quickly fed up with playing small venue gigs. I was ready for the big venues: the ones with hundreds, if not thousands of spectators.

We were getting our tour scheduled and we planned to stop in every city in Scotland, Wales and England. We'd be going in the summer months and spending the colder months of the year preparing for it all. It was difficult, dragging myself to the job centre every two weeks. It was tedious and predictable, but I needed every penny. So long as I had my baccy and food and something to read, I was sorted. I could have used some new clothes, but I hated shopping, so I could put it off until we started getting paid.

Everything was clicking in the band, with the precision of a metronome. We were a tight band, but we also had a certain something that you couldn't put your finger on – the kind of thing that kept people coming back. I was developing as a songwriter, writing catchier songs than before. I was being pushed – challenged to be the best I could be. I was extremely hopeful we'd "make it." I'd been waiting to make it for as long as I could remember, and I knew I'd put in the work with my guitar. I might have been considered work shy in other areas, but people just didn't understand the devotion I had to my guitar. It looked brand new despite the fact it had been used thousands of times. I could have played it in my sleep. My fingers had ever sensation memorised, so using my eyes was inessential.

I knew that getting Dan away from Clodagh's twin would be the best thing for him. It was clear to me that she was just a user, but he seemed to be captivated by her. He would have gone to the ends of the Earth just to hear an expression of her approval. It was sickening – love, infatuation, whatever it was.

We did a few gigs here and there, getting paid fifty quid a pop and distributing it between all of us. On those kinds of wages, I would only ever be able to replace my guitar picks. Knowing it was temporary made it slightly more bearable. The end was in sight, and it was going to be as beautiful as the fine end to a stormy day.

We managed to get hold of a tour bus. The lead singer, Mark, set it all up. I didn't know how he'd managed to pay for it or if he just knew the right people, but he got us a full-sized tour bus. It even had a toilet on board. It was a level of luxury I didn't think we'd ever get as a rock band.

The Hero that Walks Away

We were due to leave a couple of days later, so I tied up loose ends with Fiona. She looked like she was on the verge of tears when I told her I was leaving. She gave me a firm embrace and I withdrew a little from her clasp. She told me she feared for me on the road, that I had such a baby face that she worried someone would take advantage of me. Even after years of visiting her biweekly, it felt like she didn't know me at all. Still, my baby face was my best feature. It meant that I wasn't held responsible for anything. As far as she was concerned, I didn't make any wrong decisions; I was just struggling to survive in an uncertain world. She made me promise to take good care of myself and to check in with her when I got back. Most importantly, she allowed me to keep my jobseekers in place and to not have to review it in the time I was gone. I didn't know if we'd make a penny, she said. We might end up coming home early. She gave me a smile of blessing as I walked out the door, and one of those waves that feels like a goodbye forever that the person doesn't want to give. It could very well have been that. I just hoped the dole payments kept coming for as long as I needed them.

Chapter Thirty-Five

We were all set up and ready to go. We were leaving the next morning at 5am. It's not a time I would typically choose to get up at, but I was happy to for the band. The anticipation was overwhelming, and I couldn't wait to get back to the big stage. I knew that I mightn't be remembered from before; we mightn't even attract any of the same crowd. But in this new configuration, I felt like I was living my full potential, for the first time in my life.

Dan and Euan had to finish up in work that day. We already had the instruments all arranged in the bus. Nothing was holding us back or delaying us. We were unshackled, to anything but our instruments.

"I thought we were travelling fucking light, man," said , Euan, looking at all the equipment.

"You're the drummer, man, how can you talk?" laughed Dan. "We're going to be on the road for months – we're better to be prepared."

"True, at least we know we have something for every eventuality, right down to supplies for an earthquake when we aren't even living near the Earth's plates."

"Ha, ha, you're so funny," said Euan, spitting by mistake.

"At least I can keep my saliva in my mouth."

"Dan can't," Euan laughed. "How are you going to say goodbye to your girl?"

"I already did," said Dan, grumpily.

He was acting like a petulant child that was being dragged to the shops against its will – not like someone with access to a rare privilege. I made note of that. Why was he acting so complacent when we were about to take the most important step of our entire lives? Maybe he didn't view it as such, but he needed to, and promptly. I wasn't playing with someone whose heart wasn't in it.

On the day of the beginning of our tour, I got up early. I couldn't wait to get on the bus. My guitar was already waiting for me there, and I hoped no one had stolen or broken it. I've never liked leaving it somewhere that I'm not – especially overnight. But when I got to the bus, I was relieved to find everything as we'd left it. We were setting off two hours later, but I decided to just sit and wait. I was the first band member amidst us to get there, and that says a lot about someone's devotion to something.

Dan stormed in like he was in a mad hurry. He looked like he'd had no sleep and like his hair hadn't seen a comb in weeks. I didn't know what was wrong with him, but I was afraid to ask. He was one of those guys whose bad mood you don't want to get in the way of. He was volatile and I didn't know what to do. I've never been one for physical confrontation. I have thin limbs and I'm just not a fighter. He looked like he was ready to punch me, but I had no idea why. I was just sitting there, minding my own business, thinking of my dream life. I wondered why he wasn't doing the same. How could he be so angry when we were about to embark on the opportunity of our lives?

"What's wrong?" I asked.

I knew the question had to be asked; I just didn't want to be the one asking it. But I was the only one there. I didn't feel like I knew Dan well. I knew he was a sick bassist, but that was about the height of it. He didn't exactly disclose personal information to give you the opportunity to get to know him, and I wasn't a fan of that either. I became like a caveman in his presence, grunting at him as he did with me. He was no conversationalist. I could be, under the right circumstances and with the right company. He wasn't it. He plonked himself down beside me.

"Why are you here so early?" he demanded. "We aren't leaving until eleven."

"I'm just excited, I guess," I tailed off.

There was no other explanation, even though it felt like he was insisting on there being one.

"What about you?" I said, clearing my throat.

I had a frog in it that had only appeared in his presence. I wasn't comfortable with the guy at all. I was comfortable playing with him, but that was as far as it went.

"I need to talk to the guys – all of them," he specified.

"What about?"

"I'll just wait until they get here. Want to have a jam?" he asked me.

"I can't – my guitar and amp are packed up. Isn't yours?"

"No, mine is over there," he said, indicating its position on the floor with his long bassist's finger.

"Why?"

"I didn't pack it yet – in case."

"In case, what?"

"In case – you know – it stopped everyone else getting theirs in. I can always keep it on my knee if needs be."

"It's better to be comfortable if you're going to be there for the long haul."

"Oh, I'll be there for the long haul – but not in the way you think."

He was being elusive with every detail. It was irritating to listen to.

Finally, the others walked into the room, keeping time with each other's pace, as they were used to doing.

"Hey, guys, you're keen," laughed Euan.

"It's the most important day of my life," I said with sincerity.

I didn't often speak sincerely. It was frowned upon in Glasgow. Everyone talked in sarcasm and riddles, and they never took anything serious as seriously as you wanted it to be taken. Maybe that was one of the reasons I had never fully fitted in there. Maybe that was what had helped me to connect with Clodagh in the first place - her ability to be serious. I couldn't help wondering who she was with then. Had she met someone else? Was she more stable? Was she glad we'd broken up? They were all questions that were haunting me in my quietest moments, whenever I wanted to think about her the least. I might have saved her life, but I didn't know if she'd kept it since. I wasn't in contact with anyone that might have mentioned her now. If I'd heard that she'd been permanently hospitalised, it might have been reassuring, in a way. I would have felt like it was all taken care of, that I'd done the right thing. Sometimes, whenever I was in a relaxed state, her sharp blue eyes would just come into focus in my mind, like I'd seen them only a minute ago. I'd had to remove my favourite ring because every time I looked at it, I heard her voice cooing over how cute it was. It was lying in the bottom of a drawer now. I'd probably never be able to wear it again. I needed to get out of that stagnant city and away from all memory of her.

"Guys, now you're all here, I have something to tell you."

I could feel anger rising inside me before he'd even spoken the next sentence. When someone starts off like that, you know you're not going to like hearing whatever comes next and that you'll probably be impacted by it more than they are.

"I've decided I can't come on tour," said Dan.

He was doing a face that made me want to punch him. It was like feigned regret mixed with arrogant conviction.

"Why?" the others gasped.

I wasn't shocked; I was getting used to this happening. I thought of the bass player as easily replaceable anyway. There were probably a million of them waiting for a space to open up in a decent band. The others seemed distressed. Then came the barrage of questions.

"For good?"

"Why are you leaving?"

"What are you going to do instead?"

"Are you giving up playing bass?"

Dan indulged in answering all their questions. The answers were irrelevant; he was leaving and that was the end of the conversation, as far as I was concerned. I was quietly livid. It was hard to contain it. There was so much I wanted to say to him. He was acting selfishly, and he didn't even realise how much his actions affected the rest of the band; he was just pursuing his own happiness and that wasn't a friend.

"It's because of Amy," he said, blushing.

I wanted to give him a shake and tell him that he couldn't leave the band just because of a girl. They'd probably go their separate ways in a month or two and then the damage he had done to the band would be irreversible.

Anger was moving inside me like smoke moves upwards. The whole room felt suffocating too. I needed to get out of there, urgently. I got to my feet and grabbed my guitar. I put it in its case and stormed out of the studio. The air was heavy, and I had a throbbing in my temples. It felt like arteries were on the point of exploding. This was the true meaning of stress. Most people feel it about their work, allegedly. But I felt it about the band. The band was my work. It was my everything.

After I cooled down and had a smoke beside the river, I ventured back inside. Dan had already left, and the rest of the band were sitting around like pining puppies.

"We need to get over this and keep going, guys," I said, by way of a motivational speech. "We just need a new bass player – it's not a big deal."

I decided to take it upon myself to find a bassist. We needed session musician level talent. I wouldn't compromise on that. I didn't know if the others could be trusted to fulfil the requirements. They were too distracted with the distress caused by their friend's departure. I wished I could get through to them, but they were too burdened by the human condition; the one I seemed to be so gratefully lacking.

I promised everyone I'd find an adequate replacement. It might take a minute, but I'd pull it off. Whenever you're determined to save the day, you find a way to do it, however many obstacles might be placed in your path.

Chapter Thirty-Six

I got a guy to send me some demos that night. His playing was of a high standard. It was good to hear someone devoted to their craft. I already deeply resented Dan for what he had done. But I tried to redirect my energy into keeping the band on the road. I told the guy to meet us at 5am the next morning. It had to work out; there was no room for failure.

When I got to the bus, no one was there. I checked the time. I was there right on the dot, but there was no sign of anyone else. We wouldn't get far without our driver, or without a complete band, so I hoped they were planning on being punctual. People are always punctual for the things that matter most to them. I mightn't have been able to be punctual in relationships, but I was able to be right on time for my band family. I wished they could extend me the same courtesy. I was getting tired of going to heroic lengths for people that treated our business venture cavalierly.

A guy that vaguely resembled his profile picture walked towards me, hesitantly.

"Are you Matt?" I asked. "The bassist?"

"Aye, Glen?"

"Yeah," I nodded, extending my hand and shaking his.

"Glad I made it to the right place."

"Thanks for not letting us down, man."

"No problem. Maybe we can have a jam once we get on the road. I'll have to learn all the songs of course."

"Feel free to make your own mark on them. We had an average bass player before you, so the songs could do with being livened up again."

I remembered Dan for a mere moment and the tight rhythm he always delivered. He mightn't have been a virtuoso, but he was a reliable timekeeper that locked in with the drummer.

We stood in the early morning air. It might have been the beginning of summer, but it was freezing, as Glasgow often is. The sun hadn't risen to bring us warmth and we stood, our arms folded to our chests, conserving whatever heat we could – just two skinny guys.

Matt reminded me of myself, and I felt hopeful about him. I wanted the others to feel the same way, but I'd started to doubt whether they were going to show up. We sat side by side on the kerb. The cold concrete chilled my rear.

I made a joke about it and Matt laughed. I felt like we vibed well with each other. There was none of the usual awkwardness that likes to show up on first meetings.

Ten minutes passed, then, twenty, forty-five and then, one hour. It felt like my body was an ice carving. My limbs were stiff and slow to move. I didn't understand how it could be so chillingly cold on a Summer's morning.

The rest of the band didn't show up. It took a while to work that out, and several unanswered calls to confirm it. Eventually, I had to tell Matt he could go. It was harder than a break-up ever could have been, but it was probably the equivalent to one for most people I knew. I was feeling how I was meant to feel whenever I'd said goodbye to romantic partners, but my true love was my guitar and the world of fame that awaited us. It felt like we were standing, stranded on a secluded shore, watching the ship we were meant to be boarding disappearing into the distance like a dipping sun. We'd missed our chance. It was time to go home – wherever that was.

Chapter Thirty-Seven

I couldn't bring myself to talk to Matt again after that. The whole thing had been hugely embarrassing. He was a professional and our band would never return to a place of potential in his mind. His time had been wasted, as had mine. There was no point in drumming that into anyone in the band; they didn't get the importance of it all. Some people have a bit of talent, use it for a couple of years and then forget about it while they go on to find taxable income and an average life. Maybe that was the case for my bandmates. I knew it was over. They'd never redeem themselves in my eyes. I'd lost all respect for them, and I didn't bother speaking to them again.

I got a few texts from Euan, asking how I was, but I just ignored them. It was time to move on, but did I have the will to do it a third time? I remembered a conversation I'd had with Clodagh, about my dream of "making it." I'd viewed it as a given, but now it felt like it was something that could slip through my fingers.

I stayed at home. It was dull and quiet. My flatmates were working alternate shifts and sleeping whenever they weren't. I slept night and day, waking to smoke and have an espresso, but not eating much and pining the loss my prospects.

I fell into fitful sleeps, where I dreamt about Clodagh. She was falling from the window, but it ended differently each time, like my brain was working through every possible outcome. I woke up in a sweat and kicked the blankets off. Why was my brain power being wasted on something purely incidental? That was the least of my concerns – my conscious ones, at least.

I devoured book upon book when I could sleep no longer, getting lost in fantastical worlds and plot lines. I was smoking so heavily that there was barely a moment when a filter didn't touch my tongue. It was reassuring, knowing that my bad habits were still there for me. I knew I had to go solo, if I wanted to go anywhere, but I was frozen in place. It was too difficult to take on the responsibility of so great a move. It felt like I'd arrived at the place I thought was a destination and I had only found an assemblage of broken bridges there.

After a few days, I didn't get any more messages or phone calls. They had given up on me, like I'd given up on them. I knew they'd probably do their best to piece the band back together, but it would never be what it was with my songs. They'd never make it out of the studio or get another paying gig. I hoped that at least; it would have been poetic justice.

I was alone again, in my most natural state, unbothered by the choices of other humans. They were impossible to be around. Why did they always make it so untenable? People were too imperfect. I'd learnt that in my relations with them and in band life. They would never be able to live up to my expectations of them. Images of Clodagh came to my mind. I thought of her snoring, her tears, her messiness. She was as far from perfect as you could get. I mightn't have been perfect, but I was inoffensive in how I behaved. I wasn't a nuisance to anyone.

Some part of me wanted to tell her what had happened to both bands, but I had no idea why. I didn't know the first thing about her anymore. She was a stranger to me, and she lived across the sea. I didn't know why I couldn't dislodge the memories of her from my brain.

I felt too sorry for myself to play my guitar. I couldn't bear to get it out of its case. I knew it was gathering dust, but there was nothing I could do about that.

I waited and waited for an opportunity to present itself. I'd convinced myself that was all I needed. But how it would come about, I had no idea.

Day and night were one and the same. I never opened the blinds to see the difference. I was in a pit. Some might have called it depression, but I've never felt like I was capable of that feeling. It was more like a feeling of ineptitude. I couldn't bear to start another band, just to be disappointed on the point of touring. Once might have been bad luck, but twice was a trend.

You can only spend so long in your room before you start to lose touch with reality. I was playing games on my computer, but it wasn't a substitute for fresh air and fresh perspective. I needed human contact, much to my surprise. I hadn't thought of it as something essential until I'd completely starved myself of it.

I had to go to sign on, or I wouldn't have any money left to live on. I wanted to stay put, but I knew it was time to move forwards, even if it was only to get a payment I was owed. Whenever I got there, Fiona wasn't there. I asked about her, expecting to find out that it was her day off, but I wondered why she had scheduled the appointment if she wasn't going to be there. In her place was a gruff, old guy. I knew I was in trouble before I even sat down.

"Where's Fiona?" I asked him, shyly.

"She's been moved to a different post. You'll be answering to me from now on. I'm Mike," he said. The shortened version of his name didn't make him appear any friendlier or more fun.

"I can see you've been without work for a while now. Is there a good reason for that?"

"I just don't have any luck with interviews. I was touring with my band last year, but it fell apart, due to circumstances beyond my control."

"Mm hm," he said, regarding me like he didn't fully believe me.

"What age are you, pal?"

"I'll be twenty-nine next month."

"We need to get you back into something steadier. There's no point in chasing after dreams if they don't pay the bills. Maybe you could continue playing music as a hobby, but you need a day job too."

"I've tried, but it just doesn't seem to work out."

"I'll have you a job in a couple of weeks – mark my words."

I hated the guy. I wished I could beg Fiona to return to her job, but maybe there was a reason she'd left; maybe they were on to her and her facilitation of my failure to secure a job. Even if I'd been given a uniform, paid transport and a well-paid position, it wouldn't have tempted me to be fed back into the working world. It felt like somewhere you entered and never left again – at least not until you were too old to appreciate your freedom. What good was a retirement whenever you were wasting your youth on doing things you didn't want to do? It was more than that for me; it felt like working a menial job blocked me from making the progress I wanted to make in my real career. I knew I could attempt to explain it to the suit sitting in front of me, but I knew he wouldn't understand. He only understood things in terms of application forms and multiple-choice answers. I knew we wouldn't get along and I'd leave the job centre feeling undue pressure on me to secure a post in God knew what.

He flipped through my job search diary, and a look of disgust spread across his face. "Have you attended any of these?" he asked. "They sound made up."

"I'm offended you would suggest that," I said.

I was upset he'd noticed it. I was hoping he'd at least start from the week we were on instead of digging through my work history, making judgements that weren't his to make. He said I needed to bring extra evidence to my next appointment, to show I was actively seeking work.

"You're a young, healthy guy," he said, "There's no reason you shouldn't find something by next week. You just need a push to get it done."

What I really needed was space; space to allow a new band to form and to get our tour organised. I couldn't do that when my head was filled with useless figures and my hands were worn out from pointless work. I didn't want to go back there, but I knew I needed the money. I could have asked my parents to cover it, but they'd given me a long lecture after I'd left my gaming job. They didn't think it was right for them to support me as an adult. They wondered what prevented me from supporting myself. Whenever you choose an unconventional career path, why is it so difficult to find cheerleaders in your corner? If I'd got a job in the local supermarket, they probably would have thrown a congratulatory party. It was "steady work," even though it was soul destroying. You can't be an artist and live an artless life and still feel fulfilled. But people like him would never get that. They were too simplistic.

Chapter Thirty-Eight

I was walking away from my music, against my will. I'd been auditioning for weeks, to no avail. I had no time to audition either. It was depressing. I wanted to hold auditions too, to put myself at the centre of the band, but there was no time to do it. I was working a regular job. It wasn't exciting in the least. I didn't get to feed off the hum of the crowd. I didn't get to drink myself silly and perform better because of it. I didn't get to feel the familiar friends that were the strings on my guitar. It was parked – put away in its case more than it ever had been before. I just didn't have the energy to play anymore. I was sacrificing my truest love to the world of work, and who benefited from it? I was fulfilling a call centre position. Anyone could have done it. It didn't need to specifically be me. The guy in the job centre had royally screwed me over. He'd stopped me signing on, saying that I wasn't trying to get a job, so I was left with no other choice. Wherever Fiona is now, it's probably best she doesn't know what the outcome was for me. She'd be so disappointed in the system, and the automatons they'd employed since her departure.

The world's creativity was being killed off and it felt like I was part of the whole sorry show. By following the rules, I was allowing it to happen, in a way. But what other choice did I have? They'd made it impossible for me to survive otherwise. Maybe if I found the right band with the right level of commitment, it wasn't too late to survive on touring. Getting paid to play guitar was a million times easier than getting paid to perform on the phone to please customers I didn't care about. I'd never been much of a talker on the phone anyway, so it didn't exactly flow naturally when I was speaking to people. I communicate better with music than I ever have with words.

A week after I started working there, I got up from my seat, logged off and walked out. It felt liberating, even though there was no second option. I knew if I appealed to my parents for help, they wouldn't let me starve. Maybe you have to starve to find the fame and recognition you deserve. You can't reach your dream when you're sitting, hidden away in an office building, inputting data.

My dad gave me a loan. It made me glad I had a reasonably positive relationship with my parents. They had never mentioned Clodagh to me again, which felt like dodging a bullet. Maybe they just intuitively understood that I wasn't cut out for a relationship. I knew he'd never ask me to repay it, but I'd try to, whenever I'd made enough money that I could afford to part with it. In the meantime, I knew he wouldn't miss it. He was comfortably retired, so he wasn't relying on one payment being returned to him for his survival. That was the position I was in, and I knew he'd want better for me than that.

He transferred the money to me, so I didn't have to arrange to see them face to face. Unless there's a good reason to meet up – something that takes longer than five minutes to communicate, I don't see the need for it. Thankfully, he seems to be the same way. I had no time to waste. I needed to get into a band and get back on the road. I wouldn't sign on again, on principal. They'd let me down too much. I didn't need that kind of negativity tainting me.

I found an advert on a noticeboard in the university grounds. I walked around to peruse the buildings and see what I could find. Sure enough, I found exactly what I was looking for on the first noticeboard I came across. A three-piece band were missing their third piece. It sounded perfect for me: eighties inspired, guitarist and backing vocals needed, commitment essential. I tore down the ad. It was mine and I was closing off all other avenues to it, to ensure I was the one that got the gig.

I couldn't wait until I got home to make the phone call. Sadly, there was no answer. They must have been students, in class during those hours of the day. That was off-putting and made me question their true commitment to the band. But whenever I looked at the piece of paper in front of me, the wording assured me that they would give their all.

An hour later, I got a phone call from a girl with a light, airy voice. She sounded angelic and her voice was delicious to the ears. I could imagine her being a beautiful singer without hearing more than a few syllables. It was promising. I'd never been in a band with a girl before. I wasn't against the idea, but it was new to me. She spoke with gravity whenever she talked about the band. She wanted to meet me that night. She said they were in a hurry to get up and running. Their previous member had let them down for their last gig and she didn't want a repeat of that. It sounded like we were perfectly matched.

I went to the scheduled session that night with dutiful punctuality. I had my guitar case over my shoulder, the dust mites shaken off in transit. I was eager to play. My fingers were as impatient as I was. I was sitting on the edge of the subway seat, ready to jump off at the right stop. We'd arranged to meet at my stop, and I hoped they'd be waiting there whenever I arrived. It felt like no one took music seriously. I needed to not be let down.

As I came up the escalator, I felt acid climbing upwards, out of my stomach and into my airways. The ten second climb was agonising. Then, I saw her smiling face and all my concerns evaporated. She looked as angelic as she sounded and she was beaming at me, like she was extending a heavenly invitation to me, like she was saving my soul.

I walked to her side, and I nodded at the guy that waited with her. He was a big guy, and I knew he'd be a powerful drummer. Would it work with the airiness of her voice? I didn't know, but I would find out in a few minutes.

"Glen? It's nice to meet you," she said, offering me a hand to shake.

She was mannerly in an old-fashioned kind of way. I was charmed. It looked like the other band member was under her spell too.

"I'm Liliana. This is Tony. He's the drummer."

"Hi," I said, feeling myself reddening.

I was reduced to a little boy in her presence – an obedient people pleaser. I'd never felt that way before.

"We're just going to walk to the studio and then we'll see how it goes," said Liliana.

"Where's the studio?"

"It's at the top of the town. It's called Studio Split. Do you know it?"

"I've heard of it, but I've never been."

I was relieved I hadn't; I wanted an entirely fresh start with this new band. I didn't want to enter an old studio that reminded me of the death of another band.

We walked to a shiny, new looking building. It didn't have any of the old Glasgow features, but maybe it was better that way. It was like a clean slate. We walked in and we were greeted by the guy at the desk – or rather, Liliana was greeted by him. She glided across the floor with the gentle grace with which a floor length gown sweeps a ballroom. But I could tell she wasn't all lilies and whispers; she was made of hard stuff too. She was determined and that was what was needed to make a band work.

We got into the studio and there was no messing around. We got set up and didn't talk while we did it. She was singing scales before her mic was even plugged in and her voice was rich and intoxicating. It was the kind of voice that could silence a crowd with a single exhalation. I knew I was in the right place.

I played along like I'd always been there. I was glad I'd put in the work, so I was able to improvise with ease. I knew we sounded great. Tony's timing was impeccable, and he didn't outplay us either.

Liliana smiled at me, and I knew I was in. There's a smile that bandmates exchange with each other when they know something is clicking, and that was the look she gave me. It was a look I'd been waiting decades to receive.

"Wow," said Liliana whenever we finished the song. "You're good. Are you in?"

I nodded enthusiastically.

"We need to know you're committed to this. We want to make a career out of this," she said. "If you don't feel like you can show the same dedication as us to our art, you should let us know now."

"No," I said, "I can – I've been waiting to find a band as devoted as I am. It's hard to find."

"Tell me about it," said Liliana, rolling those big doe eyes of hers.

"Do you have any gigs lined up?"

"Tonnes – we're gigging several times a week – every week for the next two months. Do you think you can keep up?"

"Definitely, that sounds great."

I told them about the failed tour attempts and the disappointment that had come with them. They listened and responded sympathetically. I could tell they'd experienced the same demolition-level of disappointment I had.

We played the full set, and then we played it again, to tighten up, and again, to lock the songs in. We were there for hours, and my interest didn't wane at all. The songs were all incredibly catchy and easy to pick up. Liliana had written them all by herself. I mentioned I wrote songs too, but she didn't seem to take that on board. She was too absorbed by her own muse to bother with anyone else's. I didn't mind; the songs they were playing were better than mine, even though it was hard to admit that. Maybe they would unlock the opportunities that had so far eluded me.

We got along fine, but talking wasn't the priority. I was grateful for that. I was tired of talking for ages about nothing with bandmates and failing to practise because of it. At least they got straight to the point.

The band name wasn't what I would have chosen myself. We were called the *Earth Angels*. I had to admit, it was a fitting name for the style of music. I hoped I'd be able to content myself with it, because it was clear that Liliana wouldn't budge on it. I liked melancholic, thoughtful band names, but there was something a little too ethereal about it; about her.

After a solid three-hours playing, our time was up. We packed up in seconds and Liliana told me how much I owed her for the session. She had to pay the guy at the desk. I was surprised he charged her to be there at all, with the look he'd given her. I wondered if she went anywhere in life where she didn't receive that look. She was the type of person that could have got away with a lot, just by giving law enforcement one of her smiles.

I had everything I wanted, and I couldn't put my finger on what was wrong.

Chapter Thirty-Nine

I was getting paid to play guitar and sing back-up every night of the week. I wondered how on earth Liliana was completing her university degree whilst playing. She didn't mention it much. Whenever I asked her what she studied, she just rolled her eyes and changed the subject.

We drew huge crowds of people to the smallest of venues. There were empty pubs I never would have considered playing in that were crowded when we took up residence there.

Liliana told me she had contacts in the music industry. She was a distant relation of a famous singer, she said, but she wouldn't tell us who it was. She hated name-dropping, she said. If she made it, she didn't want to have to cite someone else's name every time she was asked about her ascent to fame. She said we'd be touring all summer, and we'd make a fortune. I admired her drive, and I felt myself being drawn in by her presence in the same way everyone else seemed to be. She had such a magnetic personality that it was impossible not to be.

It felt like everything was too good to be true. I didn't want anything to interfere with our goal. Liliana kept talking about us having "made it" like it was a sure thing. I wished I could have the same confidence she did about it. Tony didn't say much, but he followed her every command. Her soothing voice would have lulled a death row prisoner into a peaceful slumber. Her promises made you feel like you'd been given the answer to every one of life's unanswerable questions. I was entranced by her, as everyone we met was. It didn't even bother me that she stole the limelight. She deserved to be there. If she could get the attention of everyone around us, I was happy to remain in the shadows, fuelling our forwards projection without being noticed.

Liliana had the kind of face you could picture on billboards. She was born to be famous and everyone in her midst automatically became a follower. I couldn't help but fall for her, as far as I was capable. There was something about her that reminded me of Clodagh, but without the weakness and the vulnerability. She depended on no one. She was like a lone predator in a vast ocean. She might have scooped up some company on her travels, but they were only incidental to her.

Something inside me told me that we were doomed, but I just kept denying it. I'd had so many bad experiences of being in a band, that I was used to everything failing. I was used to feeling disappointed, and I'd come to anticipate the worst, but Liliana's talent and draw kept me hopeful we were getting somewhere. She could have got a drug dealer to give her a free fix; she was so persuasive. She definitely wasn't the same kind of character as Clodagh. I willed myself to forget her; to stop using her as a point of reference for everything. Why did her face haunt me so much? A relationship I'd had that meant next to nothing to me was shaping my entire reality. I wished I could erase her image from my mind and move forwards, as coldly as was characteristic of me.

Liliana secured us a record deal. I was elated. I couldn't believe we were going to be professionally recorded. Until that point, I had only ever recorded music in the studio with the loan of a tiny mic from the office. It produced a crispy kind of recording that never captured the band's true sound. But this was worth getting excited about. We were going to a big-name producer in London, and we would record our first album and start to make sales. He knew how to promote it. Liliana rattled off all the names of famous bands he'd produced, and I was seriously impressed. This was our entry pass into the world of fame. I knew if I trusted in the process, it would pay off eventually.

We had to travel to London that weekend, but I didn't care. I would have walked there on foot if we'd had to. Nothing could have kept me away. It was like the devotion of a long-lost lover awaiting the arrival of the ship carrying their one true love. They would have swum the last few miles just to get to them faster. Why must I always use romantic examples to illustrate my feelings towards band life? I get the sense that they're the only terms in which people understand the passion and dedication I feel towards the band. It's something that generally only love produces.

I kept dosing on and off. I'd seen a lot of the scenery on our way down the last time, but this time, I knew with absolute certainty that we would get to London because I wasn't alone in wanting it. Liliana chattered away in her usual way while she drove us. She took a few swigs of beer while she drove. It was alarming in a way, but it didn't feel like strange behaviour for her. She could break every rule and get away with it. She just had that confidence that carries you through absolutely everything. I didn't understand how on earth she was still awake after seventy-two hours of driving with minimal pit stops, but it seemed like her drive for success was feeding her literal driving. It was untiring and all-enduring. I turned up the music and danced in my seat. I wasn't the type to dance in general, but I was positively elated. The best day of my life was right in front of me. We would be signed, and we'd finally be famous. Everyone that had let me down band-wise would regret having given up. I was true to my word. I didn't make promises I couldn't keep. I had only ever promised myself that I would be a successful musician. That was the only promise I had ever made to anyone, and I was going to see it through.

I knew we'd have to do promotional stuff, and that was just part of the package. I didn't even mind posing for posters and for T-shirt transfers. We needed merchandise to sell at our gigs. It would fill me with pride seeing our fans wearing our faces. I had so many questions about recording that I couldn't shut up. I've never felt like that before: so inquisitive that I could barely pause to allow time for a full answer. Liliana didn't really satisfy me with any of her answers. It was hard to tell if she was being vague because she didn't know the answers or if it was because she wanted to be in charge. She was tearing down the motorway, going well above the speed limit, but she was so confident about it, I didn't worry about it. I didn't have a driving license, so who was I to comment on her driving? She was trying to get us there as quickly as possible. We were killing hundreds of miles in a few hours. Liliana sang loudly over the music playing, and she sounded a thousand times better than it. No matter how many times I heard her crystal clear voice, I never tired of it. She could have sung a nursery rhyme and made it sound like a masterpiece. I was proud to be associated with her. Tony was his usual quiet, inoffensive self. He and I took the passenger seat in shifts, so we barely saw each other. He was sleeping in the back with all the instruments while I sat next to Liliana.

"How do you know where we're going without any directions?" I asked her.

"I just feel it out. It's the same as music. It's an instinct."

"Don't you ever get lost?"

"Nope, not once," she beamed at me.

Her teeth were so white they seemed to glow in the dark. She was superhuman in every way. I felt like I was falling for her more each minute. But everyone that met her probably felt the same way. I didn't want any sort of romantic relationship with her. What we had went beyond that. We were more intimate than any boyfriend-girlfriend partnership could ever be. We were making new music together and we were ensuring it got out into the world so that other people could enjoy it. Collectively, we were all changing the world for the better. Soon we would hear ourselves on the radio and everyone would know who we were.

I took my turn in the back of the van and tried to get as comfortable I could on the pile of coats we'd made into a bed. We had limited space, so we had to have multi-functional items only. With my long legs, it was hard to get comfortable, but I was willing to sacrifice comfort for the sake of the band. Liliana was sacrificing sleep for it, so it was the least I could do.

We got to London in record time. It was amazing that we were all still alive and awake when we got there. It felt like I was finally touching the edges of a picture I'd been waiting my whole life to hold. It was so different from home it felt like it might as well have been thousands of miles away. It was going to become a new kind of home though: the home for our first album.

The guy that was producing our album was a friend of a friend of Liliana's uncle. He had been a musician too and apparently the same guy had produced an album he had made before he seriously got into the business. Liliana told me she'd heard it, and it was impeccably produced, even as a rough first attempt. It filled me with hope that this would be the right fit for us. I couldn't handle any more wrong turns where music was concerned. We had wasted enough time. I was in my thirties, and it felt like time was running out. My patient pursuit of fame had come to an end.

Chapter Forty

We wandered around London, utterly lost. We were looking at a map and it wasn't making anything clearer for us. The studio where we were told to meet Pete must have been so craftily hidden that no one would trespass there who wasn't invited. I thought that was by design. It sounded like an exclusive kind of place. Liliana had talked it up so much on the journey that I would have viewed it as being on par with heaven – had I believed in it. It was the answer to all our unspoken prayers.

Liliana walked us all over the city. We saw a few recognisable sites along the way, but we didn't take the time to appreciate them. We had one aim, and it was to find the studio. There would be plenty of time for Big Ben and Buckingham Palace once we had established ourselves there. Eventually, I wanted to have an apartment to stop off at in London, but for then, I was happy to share a van and live on the fuel of our fantasies. We walked for an hour in a loop, looking for an indication of the presence of a studio. I was sure she'd been given the wrong information. There was nothing left to see. We had seen every business in a one-mile radius. We probably knew the local business shop fronts as well as their owners did by then. It felt like a fruitless search, but Liliana showed no signs of giving up.

"Do you have directions on your phone?" I asked her. "Did your uncle give you anything to work with?"

"Yes, he told me this is the exact area. He said it would be hard to find, but I didn't think it would be as well hidden as this."

As she reached the end of that statement, her voice started to crack. She broke into the widest smile I'd ever seen and started to laugh.

"What?" I asked her. "What's so funny?"

"You two," she said. She was gasping for breath between snorts. It somehow didn't make her look any less angelic.

"What'd we do?" I asked, puzzled.

I hadn't thought there was anything funny about walking in circles repeatedly. We were all tired of walking and tired of each other, even though I wasn't tired of the band. The band was the music; my bandmates were just people that were helping me to get where I wanted to go. Maybe it made me more forgiving of them than I would have been of others. I imagined if Clodagh had snort laughed at me; I probably would have broken up with her on the spot. But for some reason, coming from Liliana, it inspired affection in me.

"You're so gullible," she laughed.

"Gullible?"

"Yeah, you'd believe anything I told you, wouldn't you?"

"What are you talking about?"

I felt anger suddenly gathering inside me.

"There's no studio here," she laughed.

"There isn't?"

"No, you guys would have walked all day just to find it wouldn't you?"

"Well, we were following you."

Tony had nothing to add to it. Unless you were looking for a solid drumbeat, he didn't have much to contribute to life in general. Maybe that was why he was easy to be around for so long. He didn't have Liliana's charisma, but he was quiet enough that he didn't get on anyone's nerves. He looked as confused as I did, but he said nothing.

"There's no studio," she laughed, bent double and clutching her stomach. "I think you gave me a stomach cramp," she howled. "I wish you could see your faces."

"This isn't funny, Liliana," I said.

I was getting enraged for the first time ever in her presence. It suddenly felt like she was all smiles with no substance behind them. Why had she wasted our time bringing us to a place, knowing there was no studio there? Why had we walked for hours, in search of somewhere that wasn't there? Was it all just an elaborate prank?

"I'm sorry," she wheezed, "It's just too hilarious. I couldn't help myself."

"So, there's no studio? And you knew there wasn't one?"

"Yeah, of course I knew. I came up with the whole thing. You two would follow a dead man into the ground."

"That's a bit harsh. We trusted you to get us to the studio. So where is it?"

"It doesn't exist," Liliana said, spreading her hands apart, like she was conjuring something. Whatever it was she was summoning up with her hand gestures, it wasn't of any use to us.

My guitar case was hurting my shoulder and I really needed to sit down. I set it on the ground and perched on it. Ordinarily, I would never sit on my guitar case, but this situation called for it. I couldn't make sense of what was happening and why Liliana found it so funny. She was laughing into her hand:

a futile attempt to cover up her enjoyment of the situation. Tony looked as confused as I was.

"I don't get it," I said, lighting a smoke.

I exhaled my words along with the smoke. It calmed me down, but not enough to fix the mess before us.

"What don't you get, Gleny?" she asked, flirtatiously.

She put her hand on my knee, like she needed to use it as a platform to lower herself to ground level, but I could see what she was doing. She was trying to butter me up before the bad news hit.

"Why we're here? What's so funny? Why we've been walking in circles for so long if there's no studio here?"

Liliana stopped giggling for a minute, like she was considering the weight of what had been done – or rather, hadn't.

"My uncle doesn't have a contact in the music industry," she confessed.

"What?"

"He doesn't know anyone. I just made that up."

"What? Why would you do that?"

"I thought it would be funny – to see the whole thing through and see your faces at the end of it."

"I can't believe this."

Tony was shaking his head too. He was giving his strong silent disapproval. We were both wasting our time, and the longer I looked at Liliana, the more I saw her falling apart at the seams. She wasn't the go-getter I'd thought she was. She was just a prankster with an immature sense of humour.

"There's no studio either – I just made it up."

"Why would you make us walk in circles for so long looking for something that isn't even there?!"

"I wanted to see how far you'd go."

"For what?"

"For the band…. For me. And here we are in London!"

"And what use is it?"

"You wanted to come to London anyway. Wasn't this your final aim? I helped you get there. Now we're here – let's make the most of it."

"And do what? There's no one waiting for us."

"I know that, but there will be. We will prove ourselves."

"Who to?"

"To everyone."

"I don't know how you're planning on doing that?"

"I brought all the equipment so we can play on the street. If that fails, we'll hunt down some record executives."

"Sounds like a failproof plan."

"You're a sarky bastard," she said, laughing.

"It's completely ridiculous and not thought through in the slightest."

"Does everything have to be planned out?"

"With this kind of thing … yes. We can't even play on the street without permission, as far as I know."

"So, we'll go to the city council… or whoever it is that grants permission for that."

I laughed at her then. I couldn't believe how delusional she was. She expected to make it big, but she didn't even know how to become a busker.

It was hopeless. I knew it in that instant. I wasn't getting anywhere in a band with her. Her whole demeanour transformed before me. I saw a different person entirely. I couldn't even remember what it was that had ever attracted me to her – that had ever allowed me to trust her with my most precious dreams.

Tony looked equally pissed off, but he didn't say a word. His silence was starting to anger me. Why was I the only one loudly protesting her botched plan, or rather, lack of one?

I followed my smoke with another, and another, sinking deeper into my guitar case. My concern for its contents was wearing off. What was the use in it? What was the purpose of any of it? I had wasted years of my life on unreliable people. I was as angry with myself as I was with Liliana and Tony. I wanted to storm off, but there was nowhere to go to. I was even dependent on her to drive me home. How had it come to this? How had I gone from being an independent songwriter to a back-up singer and player that relied on a bandmate to get around?

I knew I needed to get away from Liliana, and fast, but where was I meant to go? I had a tenner to my name and no way to get back to Glasgow. Maybe I was always meant to leave it, but not under those circumstances.

Liliana started to sing in the middle of the street, her voice carrying further than most would with a microphone. That raw talent was intoxicating, but the spell had been broken. I knew I couldn't trust her as a bandmate anymore. It was tragic really, watching that talent go down the toilet like a flushed jewel – never to be retrieved again.

I got to my feet, and I stared at her, channelling all the strength of my hatred for her into her pupils. She looked uneasy then. I'd never seen her look sheepish before, but I felt her recoil, like she was too embarrassed to look me in the eye. The colour had drained from her face. She wasn't made-up, but she'd always had a healthy glow. It was gone. Her attitude was like a ghost of its former arrogance.

I picked up my guitar and slung it over my shoulder. Then, I walked away.

Chapter Forty-One

I had no idea where I was. I knew I was in Camden Market. That was hard to miss, but I had no idea where I was in relation to anything else. There was a buzz about the place, and I knew it should have excited me, but I was too stressed out to appreciate it. Reggae pumped out of a set of speakers on the side of the road. It felt like everyone was dancing at my funeral. I had no idea where I was going to go from there, but I just knew my pride wouldn't let me return to Liliana for help. Tony was probably still there, standing by her side, like a loyal sidekick with no backbone. I wondered if he'd follow her into ruin, or if he'd have the sense to step aside before things went any further.

But then, I realised I didn't care. What happened to either of them was of no concern to me. They hadn't looked out for me and my dream, so why should I waste another second wondering about their fate? Liliana had cemented hers when she started making stupid decisions.

I wondered how I'd missed what had been so glaringly obvious. Liliana wasn't a trailblazer; she was manic. She obviously had a mental disorder. I thought of her dangerous drink driving and the fact she had no need for sleep for days on end. I'd been blinded by the excitement. She had a way of sweeping you up into it. Her energy was contagious. But I had been stupid not to realise what was really happening. I had just thought it was part of life on the road.

There were so many stalls and shops and so much activity about the place, but I couldn't afford to drink it in. It was an impediment on my journey to wherever it was I was going. I didn't know whether to head for home or to set up a life there. I was starving and I knew my tenner wasn't going to get me far anyway, so I spent half of it on falafel. I sat on my guitar case and devoured it. It felt like I hadn't eaten in days. I was unbearably thirsty too. I got a bottle of water and downed it in one. It felt like I'd neglected all my basic needs for the sake of our record deal. I'd thought I could run on excitement alone, but as it turned out, that doesn't get you far at all.

As I was sitting there, a girl with a familiar face approached me. For a minute, I froze. She had that wild hair that I could still feel in my memory, the wide smile that came out of nowhere, like sudden sunshine after an unrelenting storm. I couldn't believe it. Of all times and places, I was going to run into Clodagh then and there? Were we going to have the long-dreaded confrontation I'd imagined when her name cropped up in my mind? But the closer she got to me, the more her face came into focus. It wasn't her, after all. She just had a convincing lookalike from ten feet away. I felt a chill run through me. It felt like everything bad was converging in this one place. It was somewhere I'd always dreamt of visiting, but I couldn't enjoy a second of it. I felt far away from it in my mind, like I was dissociating from everything in my environment.

The girl didn't even look me in the face, and she walked away without a hint of recognition. Now Clodagh was in my consciousness again. It wasn't what I wanted or needed. It just fed into my feelings of failure. I sat there, in a state of surrender. I was running low on tobacco, and I didn't have the slightest idea what I was going to do next. I must have sat there for hours. I could feel my stomach rumbling and the sky had changed again and again. I'd seen dawn become dusk in increments. I'd noted every tonal change in the sky. Finally, someone took pity on me and sat down next to me.

It was a girl with hair as ginger as mine. We looked alike, I realised. We could have been mistaken for siblings, but she had a strong London accent. Her eyes were the same shade of hazel as mine and whenever she stared at me, it was a bit like looking into the mirror. I hardly ever looked into the mirror – really looked, I mean. I glanced to fix my hair or to brush my teeth, but I didn't stare myself down. It was unnerving having someone regarding me with such scrutiny. She looked happy to see me, but it was like she could read things off me that I didn't even know about myself.

"Why are you sitting here, sad guitar boy?"

"Is that my new name?"

"I just thought it was fitting, considering the fact you've been sitting on your guitar all day, and you know – you look sad."

"I'm not sad – not so much as I am defeated."

"It shows," she said. She was balanced on her haunches, and she drew cigarettes from her pocket and lit one without losing her equilibrium.

"Want one?" she asked me.

"You don't have to ask me twice," I said.

I gratefully breathed the fumes in and felt calmed by the nicotine. I mightn't have been an emotional person, but my emotions still got the best of me when I needed a cigarette. I was an addict, after all.

"What brought you here and why have you been sitting on your guitar case all day?" she inquired, sucking her smoke thoughtfully.

"It's a long story – I'm more worried about where I'm going from here."

"You can stay with me if you want."

"But we don't know each other."

"We'd get to know each other. I know what it's like to not have anywhere to go," she said, taking tobacco off her tongue with pincer fingers.

"How did you know I was sitting here all day anyway?" I asked.

"Do you see that stall over there?" she asked. She pointed to a gazebo across the way with gemstones on it.

"Yeah."

"That's my stall. My apartment isn't far from here."

"Ok, if you don't mind, I'll take you up on your offer – but just for a night or something."

"You can stay as long as you want. Do you mind cats?"

"I don't really know anything about them, but they don't bother me."

"I have a cat. He keeps to himself, but just to warn you. I know some people don't like them."

"I'd stay with a Great White right now if it'd get me off the street."

"You must be feeling stiff from sitting on that guitar case all day."

"It's pretty unforgiving. I think it's mad at me for using it as a seat."

The girl with the ginger hair, whose name I still didn't know smiled at me.

"You're so young –" she said. "I just want to look after you."

I decided not to mention my true age to her. It seemed that her supposition was more favourable to my circumstances.

"Don't you have to stay at your stall?" I asked.

"I was just packing up anyway – it's nearly five anyway."

"Is it ok there – without you at it?"

"Yeah, Gertrude at the next stall is lovely. She's watching it for me. I do the same thing for her. Otherwise, we couldn't even go to the bathroom," she laughed.

"I never thought of that. Is your apartment far from here."

"Can you see that building to the far right?" she asked, indicating its direction.

"With the green window frames?"

"That's the one."

"That's handy. You could roll out of bed and into work."

"You know – it looks thought-out, but it just ended up working out that way."

"I wish the things I didn't plan for fell into place too."

"Maybe they do," she said.

"What's your name, by the way?"

"Glen."

"Glen what?"

"Glen Ross."

"Has a ring to it, doesn't it. Is that your stage name or your real name?" she asked, smiling.

"Both."

"Mine is Jasmine – Jasmine Jones."

"Yours has a ring to it too."

"I can't take full credit for it. The Jones belonged to my ex-husband. My name was Miller."

"You don't look old enough to be married – or divorced."

"You'd be surprised how much you can squeeze into a busy decade."

"I wish mine had been as productive."

"I've never had anyone call that a productive use of time before," she laughed.

"At least you have stories to tell. I feel like I've been walking around in circles for years, attempting the same things and never getting anywhere with them."

She nodded with understanding. "Just let me pack up and then we'll go."

"I'll help you."

It was an amazing performance to watch – the packing up of Jasmine's stall. Everything folded down into a carry case after filling an entire stall. She was streamlined in the extreme. You could tell she'd done it a thousand times, honing her technique every time.

"What do you do with the stall?"

"It just stays here – it's locked down anyway – no one can move it. Hey," she interrupted herself. "Are you hungry?"

"Famished."

"Let's stop and grab something to eat."

"I don't have any money," I said, reaching into my pocket and revealing the few coins I had left to her.

"Leave it to me – I like to have someone to take care of – besides my cat, that is."

We called into a Chinese place nearby. It was a fill your own box kind of place. I filled mine with as much fried rice and sweet and sour chicken as would fit. I noticed that Jasmine took a small selection of everything exotic. She seemed like the adventurous type.

We sat at a two-seater table, opposite each other, with our knees touching below the table. It was a cramped place. The food smelled unreal though, and it tasted no less delicious. Why does food always taste its best whenever you're starved beyond thinking you have an appetite left? I found mine again and I wolfed it down. Jasmine looked at me with affection.

"You're a cute eater – you eat like a hungry dog."

"That doesn't sound like a compliment."

"Trust me – it is," she said.

She had a pair of chopsticks, and she was taking a lot of time over her food – picking up tiny bites and chewing each one for an eternity. I was getting a free dinner and a free place to stay, so I couldn't complain. Where else did I have to be anyway? I was no longer in a mad rush to get to the band's destination. I wondered what the others had ended up doing. They were probably sleeping in some bus station somewhere, waiting for a return trip home. I knew nothing would have come of Liliana's pilgrimage anyway. She was too disorganised in body and spirit – whatever impression she tried to put across.

I sat with her while she broke open our fortune cookies. I wasn't a fan of the taste, so I'd given her mine, but she seemed to be taking the whole tradition very seriously. She read her fortune to herself and kept it a secret, but I knew it must have been positive because her face lit up. Then she read mine aloud.

"Bloom where you are planted….That's touching," she smiled.

I thought it was probably just a corny saying, but maybe there was some truth to it. I'd been transplanted to this new city, and everything was already falling into place. Maybe it was what was meant to happen. I was meant to rid myself of the rest of the band, but I would thrive in a different way. I felt hopeful again. The hope that had died in me earlier that day appeared to be resurfacing, and it turned out it wasn't deceased after all.

Jasmine tucked our fortunes into her purse, like she was taking charge of mine as well. She was determined to make both happen. I was curious about what hers said, even though I have no natural curiosity about other people. I never have. My parents commented on that whenever I was a kid. They said that most kids questioned adults into a corner, but I never asked anyone about anything. I liked to source information for myself and if it didn't directly relate to me, I had no interest in it. I've always thought the world would be a better place if more people just minded their own business. What's the use of gossip? Why do people care what others are doing with their time?

I knew I was unusual in that. It was something I'd been criticised for at different points of life – for seeming disconnected and uninterested, but maybe it was a good thing too. I allowed people to have their own boundaries. I just didn't want them to cross mine either.

Jasmine and I walked side by side through the cold city night. It only took us a couple of minutes to get to her place and when we did, I was glad of it. I couldn't have stayed outside all night on my guitar case. I would have got hypothermia with the extremity of the temperature dip. That's if I hadn't got mugged first – or worse.

I was grateful to Jasmine, and I didn't often feel gratitude towards others. In my experience, we were the masters of our own fates, and we ended up having to bail ourselves out of other people's messes without aid. I already knew that wouldn't be the case with Jasmine. She just had an amazing energy about her. You could tell she wanted to do good in the world in general. She might have lived humbly whenever it came to her lifestyle, but she had plans that were exceptional.

We walked into her apartment. It was a small two bedroom on a top floor in a modernised building. It used to be a huge house, but it had been split off into different sections. I walked inside and felt right at home. After sleeping in the back of the van, it felt like real luxury, even though it was a simple place. It's funny the things that can shift your perspective.

Jasmine showed me to my room. It was made up as if she was waiting for the arrival of a guest any minute. Her cat made a quick appearance and then scuttled away behind the couch. It didn't look like it was going to be the kind of animal that got territorial about its living quarters. It was already picturing myself living there, and I didn't know why because I hadn't intended on staying longer than one night. It was just so inviting, and Jasmine was so easy to get along with. I had a bag with a few changes of clothes in it, but that was all. I knew I needed to figure out a way to get back to Glasgow again, or it not – to get back on my feet again.

I finally got a chance to charge my phone and whenever I did, I found a multitude of missed calls from Liliana. She'd left several voicemails, but I didn't bother to listen to them right away. I didn't want to have to explain everything to Jasmine. I was enjoying the fact that we were strangers to one another and that she didn't know the mistakes I'd made along the way. She was judging me based on what she'd found in front of her – nothing more, nothing less. It was refreshing.

Chapter Forty-Two

The relationship that was flowering between Jasmine and me was beautiful. I didn't think I'd ever use such a sentimental sentence, but my affection for her was greater than I knew I was capable of. She had a warm heart: something I still struggled to relate to. Her apartment was simple, but it was lovely. I felt much more at home there than I did in my own one. I realised just how much time I spent in bed, hidden away in my room, avoiding talking to anyone.

I didn't know why it was so easy to talk to Jasmine. It was like we were related without any of the issues that naturally arise with being relatives. She was highly imaginative. She could see the future in her mind's eye, and she liked to verbalise it for me, so I could share in that vision too. She said she knew I was destined to make it as a professional musician. I was just being moved away from the people that weren't supporting my dream. It was a protective mechanism, she said. I felt able to believe that whenever I looked at her. Whatever had led me to her could only be called destiny.

She painted pictures for me of the musician I would become. I could see myself on stage in sold out venues. I could hear the crowd yelling my name. I would get the recognition I deserved and there would be no one overbearing like Liliana standing in my way. Jasmine promised me that whenever I did make it, she'd be in the front row, shouting my name, like my best cheerleader. I believed her. I could see the devotion in her eyes. She needed a cause to work for. She was just that kind of person. I could tell her purpose in life was to lift others up and to enable them to achieve their fantasies. That was what gave her a sense of satisfaction.

It was funny how quickly I'd adapted to living there. What had been a one-night thing had turned into a permanent set-up without it feeling at all uncomfortable. Jasmine and I were together a lot, but she had her stall, and she was busy with that every day. Sometimes I tagged along for something to do. I was finding myself addicted to her presence – to her pronouncements about my future. Her amber eyes got so lively whenever she talked about the fame I'd find. It was intoxicating being around her whenever she spoke like that.

I felt more invested in the success of her stall than I had felt in anyone else's personal success. Maybe it was because her earnings were providing me with a protective environment in which to hone my craft. I played guitar and sang every evening, and Jasmine was an avid listener. She'd beg me to play if I ever took a night off. I found it impossible to resist her pleas. She was so sweet about it. There's another saccharine term I never thought I'd use to describe someone: sweet.

It felt like I was becoming a different person just by being in Jasmine's presence. I wanted to make her as happy as I could, without losing out on anything myself. She gave so freely that it made it easy to give back whatever I could. I wrote a song in her honour, and she made me sing it on repeat that night, all evening long. I felt like I loved her whenever she did that, but maybe it was my ego that was in love with her. It was hard not to drink in her admiration and feel like it was making me drunk.

I knew I had to line up gigs, or find a band, or both, but I didn't feel driven to do that. I was too comfortable talking about the future and being settled in the present. Nothing was pushing me to earn money. Jasmine shared everything she had with me. After she paid the bills, she gave me pocket money and I was glad to take it. She was like the sister I'd never had, and I had a sister I liked, but she was more of a "make you a meal once a month and let you fend for yourself the rest of the time" kind of sister. This was a level of devotion I couldn't have ever imagined. There was something about her maternal tendencies that reminded me of Clodagh, but without any of the accompanying drama. She didn't make pancakes like Clodagh's either. She wasn't much of a cook, but at least she recognised it and we agreed to live on oven meals and takeaways. In Camden, we were positioned in the optimal spot for great street food that didn't cost the Earth.

I accompanied Jasmine to her stall each day. The early starts didn't bother me anymore. I didn't have any evening commitments – unless serenading her with my own songs counted. That wasn't work; that was something to look forward to.

I could appreciate the craftsmanship in Jasmine's creations, but I didn't know anything about how she put them together. I hadn't seen her making anything since I moved in. She told me she produced jewellery in bulk and then took time off to focus on marketing her work and to direct her energy into selling from her stall. She was in the prime position for a high footfall of customers. I think that was why she sold enough to generate a living. She was lucky more than she was talented, as far as I could see. She was one of those people that just attracts luck, and I wanted to be close to her, so I could be in her magnetic field – so I could take some of that luck for myself. It felt like if you spent enough time in her presence, you'd become just as lucky as she was.

I've never been keen on cats, but Rufus didn't bother me in the slightest. He was likeable, really. There was something familiar about him. He was like an old soul – someone that appreciated decent music and good company. I was used to him padding around the apartment in his unobtrusive way. Sometimes, he came to sit beside me while I composed music. We were often alone together in the afternoon whenever Jasmine was making her final sales and I was waiting for her to come home so we could get dinner together. Rufus sat purring by my side. It was encouraging, knowing that he approved of my music too. I've always thought that animals have an intuitive understanding of sound. That's why they flinch when a door slams or they cower when their owner shouts. They understand the boundary that lies between good sound and bad sound, and they react instinctively. He never flinched at the sound of my singing; in fact, he looked soothed by it. That was heartening. With everything that had happened, it would have been easy to lose confidence in my ability as a musician. But he reminded me that it had just been a string of bad luck that had nothing to do with my musical abilities.

There were things in the apartment that needed to be attended to, but Clodagh didn't bother her landlord with them. She seemed to think her tenancy was dangling by a frayed thread. I had never met her landlord, but I'd heard plenty of stories about him. He sounded like the belligerent type. He probably thought he could bully her because she was a woman on her own. I couldn't draw his attention to the fact I was staying there either – even to stand up for her. If he found out I was there, it would have worsened the situation for everyone. It would have created stress for Jasmine, not to mention me.

I wondered how long ago my last bandmates had given up and gone back to Glasgow. I had never run into them again anyway. I knew if they were in London, there was a likelihood that I would have heard them performing on the street by then. I'd been to all the kinds of places I could picture becoming their favourite haunts, had they stayed, and they were never there. I did see lots of buskers. Most of them were lacking in talent and I could see why they were there day in, day out. It was obvious that they didn't have any other musical opportunities on the horizon. I didn't either, but at least I didn't diminish my talents by performing for pennies.

Jasmine came into the apartment, cheerily. She always called "hi" to me in her singsong tone. She had one of those clear voices that carries far, without being obnoxious. It was beautiful to me. So was she, even though she resembled me in a lot of ways. It was like looking in the mirror but finding my features slightly changed. Her chin lacked the dimple mine had. Her hair had highlights of yellow fanned through it. There were perceptible differences that differentiated one of us from another, but we could have been mistaken for siblings, all the same. Maybe that was why we had never crossed the line with one another: on some level it felt inappropriate. I knew I was supposed to be protective of her too. That was my payment for all the favours she had done for me.

Despite the loyalty I felt towards Jasmine, I knew as soon as I was offered a better opportunity, I'd be off like a shot. I couldn't help being that way – just like dogs can't help chasing squirrels, however good natured they might be with every other species. Some things are just engrained in you, and it's in your nature to act accordingly.

Chapter Forty-Three

My feelings towards Jasmine were transmuting into something else. The inevitable has a way of always catching up with you, even whenever you thought you were outrunning it. I wondered why I seemed to have unending patience for her, for her mannerisms and her human habits. It was like I was blind to her imperfections, or better able to forgive them because of her fanatical devotion to me.

It started with her stall. Her stall was getting on my nerves, even though it was funding my existence. I was getting tired of helping her to arrange everything in the same configuration every time. I was getting tired of the repetitive conversations she had with customers, and of the niceties they offered each other. Every conversation was the same, but it seemed like they considered themselves new and unique each time one unfurled. I hadn't thought that Jasmine was a small-talk kind of person. It was beneath her and beneath her intelligence levels, and yet, she engaged in it with her customers. I resented that. I glared at her, to let her know that I disapproved of it, but she didn't seem to pick up on the hint. She was too entranced by the high that comes from a sale, or a potential one. As the Christmas season approached, her sales were skyrocketing. I helped her to pack orders. She had orders flooding in online, as well as at her physical stall.

Her jewellery all looked the same to me. One piece was like a replica of the next and I had no idea why people praised them. They offered her pieces a kind of reverence I couldn't even get from the average person, not even daring to touch them whilst considering a sale. They were safely seated on their little plastic platforms, like pedestals before their fawning audience.

Jasmine's self-confidence was growing. I could see and feel it. Her interest in my music was dwindling. She didn't have the time, nor the headspace to consider it. She was too busy fulfilling her own orders. It was maddening that she wasn't giving me the basic things I craved anymore. I was starting to resent her stall, for stealing her attention from me. I tried to talk about it with her, but she was too distracted, and she wafted what I said away, as if it was a ridiculous proposition.

I didn't know why everything always transformed into something disappointing in the end. It didn't matter how highly I esteemed someone; they always fell from grace. But I knew it wasn't my fault. I couldn't control the behaviour of others. Their choices were theirs alone. I just needed to figure out where to go next. It was becoming clear to me that I could rely on no one, but myself. I was going to have to pursue a solo career if I wanted to make it.

As I was having that thought, everything changed again. Jasmine arrived home early. She told me she'd closed her stall early that day. There hadn't been much custom anyway. She put it down to the cold weather. She'd brought dinner with her: an elaborate three course banquet from our favourite Chinese restaurant. I almost felt tempted to forgive her for her neglect of me. She'd realised the error of her ways, and she seemed like she really did want me to stay.

"I'm sorry I haven't been as present as I should have been," she said. "I've just been preoccupied with the stall and the bills."

I nodded, understandingly.

"Maybe you could practise tonight – play some songs for me? I'm dying to hear your new ones."

"I haven't written any."

"Why not?"

"I just haven't felt inspired to. It feels like things aren't working out."

"With us or musically?"

"Both."

"No, we are fine – maybe you're just having writer's block. Everyone gets it."

I took what she said on board, knowing I'd already emotionally checked out of our friendship. I wouldn't share that piece of information with her. There were some things that were best kept to myself. I needed to start working on my plan to get away. I needed to move on to a place where I would never be forgotten or pushed aside for another project. My pursuit of fame had to be the most important thing.

Jasmine looked at me lovingly. It wasn't something I thought I'd ever understand. Where did that love come from? What made it flow out of her? Why did she feel such deep loyalty towards me?

"I love you – like a sister, I mean," she said, reddening.

I didn't say anything back. I just stared at my hands and hoped she'd change the subject.

"I know talking about feelings makes you uncomfortable, Glen. It's ok. I'm not looking for anything from you."

I breathed a sigh of relief.

"You just have such a little baby face – people can't help wanting to look after you."

"Even though I chain smoke?"

"It does look out of place. But no, it only increases my affection for you. It's your vice, but I can think of worse ones. You probably do it because you're carrying so much stress around with you."

I didn't understand what she was saying at all. I had never felt what could be described as "stressed." That was something I saw other people writhing in, that I had never been able to empathise with. You only get stressed whenever you're living with uncertainty. I have always lived with the certainty that I am destined to make it, even while others were letting me down.

I was plotting my escape from Jasmine. Her encouragement was becoming smothering. It was funny how admiration always ended up transforming into something unworkable. It always became suffocating in the end – however complimentary it might have been to begin with.

I always identified the flaws of others, quicker than they could uncover mine. I know that I have them, in theory. There are things that people view as undesirable qualities that I don't, because they don't worsen my experience of living. Flaws are only flaws to those that are bothered by them. I have never been bothered by mine. I feel lucky for that. Whenever I see people tussling with their own self-doubt and their own guilt, I realise how unencumbered I am with mine. I know I'm special in that way.

Chapter Forty-Four

I was on a roll, as far as songwriting was concerned. I was playing day and night and there were no other obligations to distract me from it. I had tens of songs. The recent ones I'd composed had a theme to them – there was a cohesiveness to them that told me they'd make the perfect album. I just needed to find the right record company to produce them. It's hard to do that without contacts in the music industry. But I think it's better to start from scratch than it is to start off standing on a stack of lies made up by those around you. I was better off starting from square one than I had been in the last band, believing in Liliana's delusions.

Whenever I got up that day, it felt like something had changed in the air. It was notably colder, but I knew it wasn't that. There was a sharp freshness in it that cut through everything. It was like whenever the wind changes direction in a film and you know that a huge plot development is coming – a rerouting that changes the course of the entire story.

I could still fit my belongings in one backpack and my guitar case. I hadn't acquired anything new since my arrival, even though I'd been there for months. I'd developed an affection for the cat, and for the apartment, and for Jasmine, until she'd let me down. But I could drop affections as quickly as I could pick them up. They didn't mean a lot to me. You could feel that way towards someone and then move on to something new. The only thing that's consistent in life is the fact that change occurs. There's no point in fighting it; I like to initiate it whenever I can. That's what makes me so adaptable.

We had what felt like an intimate dinner – not in a lover sort of way – just in a close sibling way. It almost felt like we had a twin-like connection, but the feelings on her side were much stronger than on mine. We ate duck spring rolls, beef chow mein and banana fritters, and I knew Jasmine thought she was repairing everything – as if some good food could make everything as it was before. That state can never continue. It always ends, whenever I see the humanity in the person that's facing me across the shared table. Still, I enjoyed the meal. It was my favourite Asian restaurant, and it would always have a special place in my heart – or stomach, like the French café on Clodagh's street. When it closed down, it marked the end of an era for all of us. It's best to get out while everything is still open. You don't want to be the last one left standing at the doorway of the vacant lot that used to hold your life.

Rufus came over to me and purred, pushing his cheeks against the back of my hand. I obliged and stroked him. He looked satisfied. He cosied up to me and put his paws on my knee, like he was claiming me as his own. Had he understood, maybe I would have told him that I had never been anyone's – nor would I ever be. I was a person that belonged to music – not to other people – or animals.

Jasmine took it upon herself to open my fortune cookie for me. At first, I might have found that charming, but now it seemed like she was crossing a boundary. Whatever my destiny was – it had nothing to do with her. It felt like she might contaminate it, just by putting her own spin on it.

"All your hard work will soon pay off," she read aloud.

Her face brightened. Had I had human feelings, that might have touched me. I didn't understand her investment in me. What was it to her? Did she think that she would ride on the coattails of my success whenever I finally made it? Calling herself my benefactor? I was deeply suspicious of her intentions. She seemed pure of heart, but so had Clodagh. People like that never make it far in the world. I thought again of Clodagh and her life back in Ireland. I wondered what it had become. I could be certain of one thing: she'd still be pining the loss of what she thought we once had. She was sentimental like that, and she didn't recover from anything easily. I felt like shuddering at the thought of her touch, or Jasmine's, or anyone's. I didn't want anyone to be near me, including the cat. His intrusion onto my knee was making me increasingly uncomfortable. I nudged his paws off.

"Aw, poor Rufus," sang Jasmine. "He was happy there."

"I wasn't – his claws were digging into my leg."

"Oh, fair enough," said Jasmine, giving me a second and third look.

I felt like she was trying to analyse me – like she wanted to read my mind, but I would make sure I was unreadable. I didn't want her to delve into me and try to work out what I was. She might have thought she had access to the depths of my soul, but I knew I didn't have one. I didn't have any "depths." I was all shallow thought and ambition. That was my driving force.

There are so many people in the world that want to think the best of everyone. They find things in strangers' characters that were never there to begin with. Jasmine and Clodagh are two prime examples of that type of person. They think you have a good heart, and your goodness just needs to be drawn out – like it has retracted like a tortoise's head inside a shell, only for self-protection. That isn't the case, nor has it ever been the case with me.

There is no heart in me. The problem is that people like Jasmine have such big hearts they couldn't conceive of someone not having one. They keep putting themselves out there, trying to draw you out of your tortoise shell, but you were never hiding anything to begin with. Why can't they just take you at your word? Sometimes there is no hidden meaning – what you see is what you get. A baby face can distract you from the truth, but it's just a face – an outer coating that covers up a rotten inside.

While I was having all those thoughts, Jasmine was regarding me with interest. She had her chin cupped in her hand and she leant her elbow on the table. There were takeaway bags everywhere – torn into like hungry animals had got into them. Maybe that was all we really were.

"Did you enjoy your dinner?" Jasmine asked.

"Yes, I did, thank you."

"You don't sound too enthusiastic about it."

"It was as good as it always is."

"How are you so cool and collected all the time – I get the sense that no matter how long I live with you, I will never really get to know you."

She had finally uttered a truth about me – although she wouldn't be able to recognise that. It was probably just a flippant remark – something she gave no more thought to than any other utterance that came from her mouth.

She had a grain of rice stuck to her face, but I didn't bother telling her, even though it was annoying me. That was her embarrassment – not mine. I hadn't said anything positive to her, so I didn't see the point in saying something negative, even if it was for her sake. We were alone in the apartment anyway, and I knew Jasmine wouldn't go out again that day. She was in for the night, and she thought that everything between us was repaired. What she didn't know was that there wasn't really anything to break in the first place.

I slept in my bed there, mainly because it was more comfortable than leaving. Where else would I go after dark with very little money? I needed to do whatever was most beneficial to myself. I couldn't just walk out, even if I felt like I was finished with Jasmine. In a way, she had created a comfortable trap for me. The cat was in my bedroom, plucking the duvet and making itself a cosy nest. I left it there. I didn't want it there, but I was able to ignore it. If only I was able to ignore people's annoying habits as easily. It would have made it much easier to sail through life, putting up with the people I was forced to be around. Then again, maybe if I'd been a different, more tolerant kind of character, I wouldn't be the musician I was. Sound was the most important thing to me, so I took the bad with the good.

The following day, I woke up with a renewed sense of gratitude to Jasmine for what she'd done for me. She wasn't a relation of mine, even if it felt like she was. Her ginger hair didn't come from the same source as mine. She was just a kindly stranger – one that had made me into a friend. I decided to accompany her to work that day. Maybe she could use an extra pair of hands. I was trying – trying to be the kind of friend I knew I should be. I'd seen it practised by so many others in my time. It was easy to replicate it – for a day, at least.

It was lucky I went with her because she had an incredibly early start. I couldn't understand why anyone would want to buy jewellery at 8am, but apparently, they did. She was inundated with orders, both in person and online. While she was attending to customers on her phone, I tried to minimise the stress for her by serving the customers in our physical vicinity. There was sale upon sale. Thankfully, the fact her stall was so predictably laid out meant that I knew exactly what to do. There were no questions I needed to ask Jasmine. She was lost in her phone – like she was living in another world entirely. I knew she was still working, so I did what I could to be of service to her. I had no intention of making it a regular thing, but I suppose it was my half-hearted attempt at paying her back for her generosity.

I bagged the items, robotically. I didn't pay much attention to the craftsmanship of them. That wasn't my domain. I just knew how to serve people, even though I would have resented doing it for a daily wage. It was cold standing there all day, but Jasmine had brought us flasks of tea and pairs of gloves. She put some on me. They were too tight for my long-fingered hands, but it was better than having hands like ice. The customers were mostly friendly that day. I knew from Jasmine's stories that they could be a mixed lot. Whatever way they were with her, she just had to suck it up and take it, if she wanted to make sales. She was good at that. She's a passive sort of creature that doesn't offend easily. Maybe she needed to be that way to take me in in the first place.

I stayed on my feet all day, never getting a break from serving. It must have been because of the approaching Christmas season; everyone was feeling generous and gifting jewellery to their loved ones. Several passersby fawned over the jewellery but didn't buy anything, but that was just par for the course. I knew that Jasmine didn't let that kind of thing settle under her skin. She just kept moving forwards in her positive way, no matter what might have knocked her. She was resilient in a way, I thought. Maybe if I left her side, she'd survive just fine. She might just go on to look for her next charity case. She seemed like the type of person that lived for that kind of thing. I could never relate to that, however much I considered it. It was just so alien to me and to the person I was.

We had some soup for lunch – minestrone that Jasmine had made herself. I didn't know how she squeezed so much into a day without ever looking ruffled. It all just came so naturally to her, like notes come from the strings for me. We all have different gifts, I suppose – no matter how flawed others might consider us to be.

The torrential downpour came after lunchtime. Gladly, we were sequestered under the reliable hood of Jasmine's gazebo. She had camping chairs she put up for us, so we could find some comfort there. Custom dwindled then. The weather chased the customers faster than a sign reading "closed" ever could have. We were glad of the lull. Jasmine had time to catch up on checking her orders online. They were flooding in. She was a huge success, whether she viewed herself as such or not. She had created this business from nothing and put her whole being into it. I didn't know how she had anything to spare for me, but somehow, she did.

I offered to go and get us coffees from the neighbouring coffee van. They'd been busy all day too, but the queue had vanished, and the aroma of coffee was so inviting. I wondered if that feel was what made people stay in their cosy houses, refusing to go out into the big, cold world, seeking opportunity and excitement. Even though I could appreciate it in that moment, I could never live that kind of quiet life with satisfaction. I was always restless, always wanting more than I had in front of me. As I carried the two coffee cups back to Jasmine, I noticed something terrible happening. Whoever had the bright idea had waited for an opening – for her to be alone, to make their move.

The money box was sitting on the tabletop. It wasn't locked; the key was in the lock. Jasmine didn't bother putting it away because she always needed change for her cash sales. She didn't religiously empty it either. It was filled to the brim with her cash earnings from that whole week. She just took it for granted that it was safe there. It always had been, so why wouldn't she? Still, I don't see the best in people the way she does, so to me it seemed like an act of trusting stupidity.

Someone snatched the money box. She protested, but they forced her arm away, pushing her back into her seat. They were masked, but they had a recognisable frame. They were unusually tall with eyes of emerald. I didn't think they'd be hard to identify in a line up, but it didn't put them off. They grabbed the box in both hands and started to run. I dropped the coffees to the ground and chased them down. They were making a break for freedom, but I wasn't going to allow it to happen. Jasmine's livelihood was in that box. Mine was too. It equalled hundreds of hours of loving work on her part. I shoved the thief to the ground and jumped on top of him, pinning him down. Several of the other stall holders came to my aid. One grabbed the money box from his grip. Another phoned the police. I sat on him, putting all my body weight into keeping him in that one place. He was trying to fight me, but he was in the position of submission, so he couldn't move an inch.

"Get off me, you fucking dickhead," he spat, in his cockney accent.

"If you think I'm moving, you're even more of an idiot than I thought," I said.

Stealing a money box in broad daylight did seem like a pretty idiotic thing to do, but he had been dangerously close to making off with it. I can't watch anyone getting away with things they don't deserve. I've had to endure enough in terms of wasted time in directionless bands. Why should money fall into the hands of someone that doesn't even try to make it on their own?

Sirens wailed and the police came to my aid. I got up from the ground and let them arrest the thief. They pulled his mask off so I could look straight into his face. I knew his face. I was surprised I'd missed the emerald glow in his eyes before. He was a regular at the market. He was always doing the rounds, looking everything over but never buying anything. He must have been scouting out the riches to be found there.

I watched him being taken away to his punishment. He deserved every bit of it. I didn't feel any remorse, but I basked in the praise that came from the other stallholders. They were so impressed by what had happened, but I'd just acted on instinct. Some people work well under pressure, and I am one of those people. Maybe I even need it applied to me to get me to achieve something.

That thought was what precipitated the next day's events. Jasmine and I packed up after that. It felt like we'd dodged a bullet, and we didn't want to tempt fate any further.

"I'll have to empty this now," she said, carrying her money box like it was her childhood memory box. Something she'd been cavalier about had suddenly become extremely important to her. Sadly, I couldn't say the same about myself. I still felt as hollow as I had before the incident. I had made sure justice was served, but I had no real feelings about it. I wasn't sad, or shaken up, or troubled. I just moved on to the next moment, the way I always manage to do.

Chapter Forty-Five

The next day was a strange one. I awoke much earlier than usual. Jasmine wasn't awake yet. I realised I must have adapted to her sounds of waking. Even whenever I didn't get up, I was conscious of her leaving for work, of the sounds of the apartment that had become familiar to me – the crunch of the cat food between Rufus's teeth, the sound of running water in the bathroom, the radiators filling with gurgling heat. None of it made me feel at home, even though it was probably meant to. I was still homeless in my mind. It doesn't matter how much of a semblance you present of being settled, if you don't feel it, it's all a charade. You can only pretend to be someone you aren't for so long. Eventually the mask starts coming apart at the seams and whatever is behind it becomes visible. I like to get out before that happens. It's better to leave on bad terms with someone still thinking highly of you. I prefer to be on a pedestal than to be a piece of dirt on the ground, but who doesn't? At least through the medium of this book, I can be honest about my true intentions, and I don't have to hear the echoes of disgust.

I got dressed and packed my bag. I got my guitar and set it next to my backpack at the door. I had to wait for Jasmine to get up. She was sleeping late because of the previous day's drama. Her self-imposed day off was what she needed most. I knew she needed to rest, so I didn't attempt to wake her. I just waited patiently in the living room, tossing a tin foil ball for the cat and looking around at the furniture. I didn't feel any attachment to it, even though I'd been there for a long time by then, and it was the closest thing I had to a home.

Finally, Jasmine got up. She looked disorientated when she did. She looked from me to my bags, to me, to my bags, questioningly. She was still rubbing the sleep from her eyes. I knew it was going to be a shock for her, but it was best to burst the blister now, instead of leaving it to get rubbed for weeks, hurting so much more before it inevitably bursts by itself.

"What's happening Glen?"

"I'm leaving."

"Where will you go?" she asked, cocking her head like she was talking to someone unhinged, someone that might lash out any minute.

I had dealt with that before, as you, reader, know. So, I knew without a shadow of a doubt that I wasn't that. I couldn't have been thinking more logically than I was in that moment.

"I'll figure it out."

"So, you aren't going to tell me?"

"I don't know, Jasmine. I'll see where the wind blows me."

"Aren't you afraid?"

"Afraid of what?"

"What you'll do next?"

"Things always have a way of sorting themselves out. Look how I met you."

"And much good that was to me," she said.

There was a bitter undertone to what she said, like the unpleasant tang of an underripe raspberry. It was uncharacteristic of her, but then again, I'd never put her in this position before. People are capable of behaving vastly differently in different circumstances. I couldn't condemn her for that. Knowing her had brought me a lot of goodness – until it had stopped. It always stopped, whoever the person was – so why did they always take it so personally?

"Why did you go to such lengths to help me yesterday?"

"I had to – I have to right injustice."

"Isn't this unjust?"

"Not to me – no."

"I thought you'd stay for good."

"There was never a contractual agreement between us. There was no lease – no obligation."

"What about the obligations that come with friendship? What about emotional obligations?"

"I don't know what those are," I said. There was nothing else to say – nothing that would ever satisfy her anyway.

Chapter Forty-Six

I'd walked out of the apartment less than five minutes after that conversation took place. Jasmine hadn't hugged me goodbye or offered to help me to carry my belongings downstairs. The exit was much more unfriendly than the entrance, but isn't that always the case? I don't think that's unique to me and how I interact with people.

I was walking on a street I knew well by then. I only knew pockets of London: the places Jasmine had taken me to. Mostly, I knew Camden like the back of my hand. I mentally toyed with the idea of setting up a stage somewhere in the market, finding somewhere to showcase my songs. But I would have been fighting with the recorded music blasting from speakers in shop fronts. Truthfully, I knew it was beneath me anyway. Busking was lower than what I was aiming for. It was on par with cleaning out dustbins as opposed to having a cleaner take care of the dirt for you. You can't aim low and expect to reach the stars.

I could see my face printed on one of them in my imagination, like the Hollywood stars so many successful people before me had dreamt of. I could see myself being added to them. It just felt like it was where I belonged. Maybe I'd always been a fictional sort of person – a character rather than real flesh and bone. I've always been better with the imaginings I come up with than with life's dirtied realities. People are messy. They can't just live in neat boxes like I wish they could. I can handle a certain amount of mess on the road, for the sake of the band, but not in my personal life. I don't need any emotional upheaval. I've never been able to relate to it.

These insights into my character are as new to me as they are to you. I never take the time to look inward; I just don't see the point in it. I don't want to try to change who I am. Can any of us really ever do that anyway? It's a lot of hard work, and for what? For other people's benefit? People will always come and go for me.

Chapter Forty-Seven

I ended up sofa surfing after that. Thankfully, Jasmine had topped up my phone for me, so I was still able to contact people. Whenever I needed to use the computer, I went to the library. Jasmine had insisted upon me getting a library card too. She said you never knew when you might need it, and she'd been right about that. Had she known that signing me up for one would make the process of disengaging from her easier, maybe she wouldn't have been as quick to sell it to me.

I knew she'd probably be beating herself up by then, for whatever she had done to fail me, as if anything she could have done would have changed the outcome of it all. At least I knew she had her stall. She was a survivor. She wasn't another Clodagh. She would keep selling her art and she'd probably find someone new to look after. The maternal instinct in her couldn't resist doing that. I'd eventually be forgotten, apart from in passing thoughts – ones where she tried to make sense of me and couldn't. Nobody could do that – not even me. At least I hadn't let her down completely. I'd been of service to her the penultimate day. If I hadn't been there, she would have lost all those earnings. At least I got to be a bit of a hero before I walked away.

For years after that, I moved from place to place, from sofa to sofa. Some were soft and satisfying – others had broken springs and caused back pain. I went to every major city in the UK. I played in as many bands as there are days in a year. I've forgotten most of their names now. Everyone has. They never got their dream off the ground. I didn't either, but maybe if I'd been surrounded with less incompetence, I would have made it by now. I lead a quiet life, but I haven't given up. I will never rest until I get what I deserve; fame, popularity, monetary reward for the years I've sacrificed to my guitar – to the pursuit of my musical ambition. I can be brave when the occasion calls for it – momentarily. An innocent face and bursts of bravery when required can get you quite far in this world. I mightn't be able to love people – at least not in the traditional sense of the word – but at least I have my guitar. That's all I need: my guitar and my smokes and I'm happily on my way.

Printed in Great Britain
by Amazon

36785171R00093